*The Ongoing Struggle*
*Volume I*

# CROSSROADS

**BRENDA S. JACKSON, PH.D.**

FOREWORD BY
Rev. Dr. Audrey Turner

*Priority*ONE
publications
Detroit, Michigan, USA

Cross Roads: The Ongoing Struggle
Copyright © 2012 Brenda S. Jackson, Ph.D.

All scripture quotations, unless otherwise indicated, taken from the HOLY BIBLE, NEW INTERNATIONAL VERSION®. NIV®. Copyright© 1973, 1978, 1984 by International Bible Society. Used by permission of Zondervan. All rights reserved.

Scripture quotations marked (KJV) are taken from the HOLY BIBLE, KING JAMES VERSION (Authorized).

Scripture quotations marked (NASB) are taken from the New American Standard Bible®, Copyright © 1960, 1962, 1963, 1968, 1971, 1972, 1973, 1975, 1977, 1995 by The Lockman Foundation. Used by permission. (www.Lockman.org)

Scripture quotations marked (LB) are taking from the Holy Bible, New Living Translation, copyright © 1996, 2004, 2007 by Tyndale House Foundation. Used by permission of Tyndale House Publishers, Inc., Carol Stream, Illinois 60188. All rights reserved.

Scripture quotations marked (NRSV) OR (RS) are taken from Revised Standard Version of the Bible, copyright 1952 [2nd edition, 1971] by the Division of Christian Education of the National Council of the Churches of Christ in the United States of America. Used by permission. All rights reserved.

All poetry submissions herein are © 2000 – 2012 Brenda S. Jackson

All rights reserved. No part of this publication may be reproduced, stored in a retrieval system, or transmitted in any form or by any means – electronic, mechanical, photocopy, recording, or any other – except for brief quotations in printed reviews, without the prior permission of the publisher.

*Priority*ONE Publications
(800) 596-4490 Nationwide Toll Free
E-mail: info@p1pubs.com
URL: http://www.p1pubs.com

ISBN 13:     978-1-933972-22-0
ISBN 10:     1-933972-22-X

*Edited by Patricia A. Hicks*
*Cover and interior design by PriorityONE Publications*

Printed in the United States of America

# TABLE OF CONTENTS

Preface .................................................................................................. 4

Foreword        Reverend Dr. Audrey Turner ................................................ 5

Seminar #1     The Ongoing Struggle ............................................................ 9
               The Spiritual Struggle
               The Holy Spirit

Seminar #2     Alone in a Crowded Fishbowl ............................................. 47
               Loneliness
               Sermon

Seminar #3     Fear and Faith ..................................................................... 67

Seminar #4     Training Up a Child While Incarcerated ............................. 79

Seminar #5     You Shall Not Murder (Suicide) .......................................... 95

Seminar #6     Agape ................................................................................ 107

About the Author ............................................................................... 147

## PREFACE

We experience the Cross as we journey through life. This experience includes suffering, but we remember we have already received the victory of the Cross from Him Who defeated sin through the Cross. Life is full of crosses, and we can be victorious over them all. This book is to help us identify our Cross experiences and to stay on the right road to victory.

# FOREWORD
## Reverend Dr. Audry L. Turner

Dr. Brenda Jackson and I have known each other for more than 20 years. We were matriculating at William Tyndale College (Farmington Hills, MI), where we were introduced to one another by a mutual friend, the Rev. Stephen Byrd (now deceased). At that time, we were both working on a second Bachelor's Degree to advance our work for the Lord and in pursuit of strengthening our philosophical and theological perspectives.

Currently, Dr. Jackson and I are members of the Council of Baptist Pastors of Detroit and Vicinity, Inc. (CBPDV); where I serve as Assistant Secretary/Lecturer and she as a Member/Lecturer. Over the past five years I have served as Event Manager of the City-Wide Revival in Detroit, sponsored the CBPDV and City of Detroit Health Department, Prevention and Intervention Substance Abuse Program. Dr. Jackson and I were responsible for coordinating more than 30 evangelists for the Revival's Evangelism Team. The team presented the Gospel of Jesus Christ to the ex-prisoners who were transported to the revival, and more than 50 accepted Christ Jesus as Savior.

It is through the grace of God that Dr. Jackson is launching another seminar for prisoners who are experiencing ongoing spiritual struggles…road crosses. In the past, Dr. Jackson has given lectures referencing her publications for the purpose of equipping pastors, preachers and lay people on how to minister to those who are incarcerated. Today, Dr. Jackson is as authentic as she was then, passionate and empathetic in her work for the Lord to help prisoners. She is fulfilling her God-given calling to help prisoners on earth as it is in heaven, digging deeper and deeper into this treasure in earthen vessels to help not only those who are or were in prison, but those who believe they are called to work with prisoners. It's apparent that she does not do this work for her own glory but for the glory of God Almighty. Consequently… excellency [greatness] of the power may be of God and not in Dr. Jackson [us] (II Corinthian 4.7).

It is my pleasure to know such an amazing, awesome woman of God who loves to minister to prisoners and others. Currently, Dr. Jackson is working on her second doctorate degree. When were in undergrad, we would visit jails to preach and teach the Word of God to those who were in need of a Word from the Lord or an affirmation of hope in spite of being incarcerated.

I minister to prisoners and ex-prisoners continually, as does Dr. Jackson. She and I assist ex-prisoners in their transition back into society and connect them to churches upon their return home. We have sought to familiarize ourselves with the struggles that ex-prisoners and prisoners endure in their return home, and while in prison, i.e., loneliness, grief, losses, anxiety, isolation, separation, anger, pain in their hearts that lead them, in most cases, to criminal activity. We can also relate to the spiritual, emotional, physical, mental challenges they may face.

Prison ministry is indeed a labor of love for Dr. Jackson. She is not financially compensated for what she does, however, her greatest reward is to catch sight of a lost soul that becomes saved, sanctified and filled with the Holy Ghost, until she sees Jesus for her greater reward in heaven.

**The Ongoing Struggle Volume 1** is her newest publication designed to help prisoners discover how to handle the ongoing spiritual struggle(s) occurring deep within. She challenges the readers to accept and receive their help from the Holy Spirit. Empathically, she teaches and preaches in this seminar that it is the power of God through the Holy Ghost that rebuilds, habilitate, or restore the lives of prisoners once Jesus is accepted as their Savior and author and finisher of their faith. Dr. Jackson points to the effects of fear. Fear is an enemy that is in operation when one's faith fails; it will kill, steal and destroy us if we will not turn to our Helper, Creator and Maker, God almighty. This seminar is written in a simple and easy-to-follow format. When we were students at William Tyndale College we were taught to keep the Gospel simple; at a level a child can understand it. You can see this simplicity in her seminar.

The process that Dr. Jackson presents in the seminar is validated in the lives of transformed prisoners and ex-prisoners who are either in prison or have returned home. Those that have returned home have not recidivated; they are productive citizens in their communities, homes, jobs and churches. These individuals realized that their fight is not against flesh and blood but against principalities, against powers, against the rulers of darkness… in high places (Ephesians 6.12). This ongoing struggle is not only experienced by prisoners, but prisoners' of sin. Dr. Jackson addresses real-life issues that prisoners face while incarcerated; what she has been exposed to first hand or witnessed while ministering to them in their abode (prison bumps).

If you need to be rescued from your ongoing struggle(s) of this old world, then this seminar is indeed a self-help session. It not only deals with what the prisoners experience in their interpersonal skills or ongoing struggles in and out of prison, but it presents an opportunity for the prisoner to raise or train up their children while incarcerated. The children of prisoners are affected/effected by their parents' incarceration. In some cases, it may be generational curses that have been transferred from generation to generation. Also, the emotions, spiritual, physical and mental capacities of the incarcerated parent and child/ren must be taken into consideration for rebuke and correction to produce productive citizens and Christians in our communities, city and state.

All behaviors are learned, therefore, in order to become spiritually transformed the mind, body and soul must be renewed by the power of the Holy Spirit and the studying of the Word of God. Seeking forgiveness from a child/ren is indeed in order to set the soul free from guilt and shame. Spiritual formation for incarcerated parents can be transferred to their children, just as their unacceptable behaviors were transferred. Dr. Jackson challenges participants to establish a solid family reunion through the work of the Holy Spirit; to adopt positive parenting skills as illustrated in the Bible; to train up a child while in prison in the way of the Lord through solid instruction.

Lastly, Dr. Jackson confronts participants at the seminar not to commit spiritual suicide; that is, to not reject Jesus Christ as Savior or "Suffering Suicide," the deliberate act of killing self through despair. She provides preventive measures for suicide and promotes God's inner peace as the prisoner's protective custody.

In my work as a former Church Coordinator for Transition of Prisoners, Inc., I matched more than 100 ex-prisoners with mentors in various ecumenical churches throughout the city of Detroit. I am humble to say that those persons are now productive Christians and citizens in society. Additionally, as a certified Mentor Trainer for ex-prisoners; I've trained more than 200 mentors -- and continue to do so. Clearly, Dr. Jackson and I are acquainted with the spiritual struggles incarcerated persons are experiencing in their lives. Dr. Jackson I have been devoted to this work. Albeit is not without struggle, but similar to the incarcerated, Dr. Jackson and I must continue the good fight of faith to keep hope alive for those who feel hopeless.

Our motto at Nehemiah Baptist Church (where I serve as the Senior Pastor, Teacher and Pastoral Counselor of the Gospel of Jesus Christ) is "No Soul left Behind." I, Reverend Dr. Audry L. Turner, conclude that the seminar _Ongoing Spiritual Struggles_ is precisely what incarcerated persons need to contend with the spiritual struggle(s) within. Without the power of the Holy Spirit in their lives they can do nothing on their own.

I am in awe reading this material. I am anxious to see how God will work with the readers seeking help from the Holy Ghost; as they (the incarcerated) come up out the hole Satan has dug for their souls…road crosses.

Yes, I want to witness the Lord our God using those who are "Called" to help the incarcerated employ Dr. Jackson's seminar _Ongoing Spiritual Struggles ... Road Crosses._

*Seminar 1*
# THE ONGOING STRUGGLE

BSJ Christian Seminars
Minister Brenda Simuel Jackson, Ph.D.
© All rights reserved.

## THE ONGOING STRUGGLE

© Brenda Simuel Jackson

The war is on, will it ever end.

The battles are not new, there seems to be a trend.

Pornography is not just in magazines,
the internet highway provides several different bins.

The flesh continues to crave the things that reprobation raves.

The thoughts of our mind travel a dark road,
but light is somewhere for us to win the gold.

The anger in us is used by the enemy to our destruction.

Self-control is a weapon we must use so escape is constructed.

How do we fight this never ending battle?

We must stand, resist, and make right choices, not get caught like cattle.

Living godly requires cultivation of our spiritual fruit.

Winning battles requires godliness that increases even if we must reboot.

## SEMINAR OBJECTIVES

The Participant will understand:

- The inner spiritual struggle
- The external spiritual struggle
- The differences between physical and spiritual battles
- The enemies
- How to gain victory
- The Person of the Holy Spirit

# FOUNDATIONAL SCRIPTURES FOR THE SEMINAR

1 Timothy 4:7, 8 (Amplified)
"But refuse and avoid irreverent legends (profane and impure and godless fictions, mere grandmothers' tales), and silly myths, and express your disapproval of them. Train yourself toward godliness (piety) [keeping yourself spiritually fit.]
For physical training is of some value (useful for a little), but godliness (spiritual training) is useful and of value in everything and in every way, for it holds promise for the present life and also for the life which is to come."

Galatians 5:22-24 (Amplified)
"But the fruit of the [Holy] Spirit [the work which His presence within accomplishes] is love, joy, (gladness), peace patience (an even temper, forbearance), kindness, goodness (benevolence), faithfulness;
gentleness (meekness, humility), self-control (self-restraint, continence). Against such things there is no law [that can bring a charge].
And those who belong to Christ Jesus (The Messiah) have crucified the flesh (the godless human nature) with its passions and appetites and desires."

Ephesians 6:10-12ff (Amplified)
"In conclusion, be strong in the Lord [be empowered through your union with Him]; draw your strength from Him [that strength which His boundless might provides].
Put on God's whole armor [the armor of a heavy-armed soldier which God supplies], that you may be able successfully to stand up against [all] the strategies and the deceits of the devil.
For we are not wrestling with flesh and blood [contending only with physical opponents], but against the despotism, against the powers, against [the master spirits who are] the world rulers of this present darkness, against the spirit forces of wickedness in the heavenly (supernatural) sphere."

# SPIRITUAL BATTLE ASSESSMENT

1. Do you have an ongoing problem you are unable to solve?

2. When did this problem first present itself?

3. Describe your relationship with the Lord during this time.

4. Did anything happen during this time that convicted you?

5. Was there an urge to do things you knew you should not?

6. Were there unwholesome thoughts that continually plagued you?

7. What were the temptations you faced?

8. Describe those things you did not believe you had control over?

9. What solutions did you try?

10. Was the problem(s) solved?

11. How? Or why not?

Assess your battle(s) by analyzing your responses. Share your analysis with a confident believer.

# KEY DEFINITIONS

Spiritual Warfare as defined by June Hunt:
> "Ongoing conflict against the human race with its enemies - the world, the flesh, and Satan." (Hunt, 1)

Spiritual Warfare as defined by Dr. Clinton and Dr. Hawkins, psychologists:
> "A struggle between light and darkness." In biblical terms light is good and dark is evil. (Clinton & Hawkins, 239)
> Results of Spiritual Warfare:
> - Keeps non-Christians from coming into a personal relationship of faith within and in Jesus Christ.
> - Stops the effectiveness of true Christians.

Spiritual Strongholds:[1]
> Deeply rooted thought patterns with three main characteristics:
> - Worldly thinking
> - Fleshly habits
> - Satanic influences

Spiritual:[2]
> - Nonmaterial
> - Spiritual body
> - Spiritual things
> - Spirit references good and evil spirits (Youngblood, Bruce, Harrison, 1198)
>   - Not God
>   - Not human

---

[1] 2 Corinthians 10:3-4 (Amplified): "For though we walk (live) in the flesh, we are not carrying on our warfare according to the flesh and using mere human weapons. For the weapons of our warfare are not physical [weapons of flesh and blood], but they are mighty before God for the overthrow and destruction of strongholds."

[2] 1 Corinthians 15:44b (Amplified): "...there is a physical body, there is also a spiritual body."

Demons: (1 Peter 3:19-20; 2 Peter 2:4, Jude 6)
- Group of fallen angels
- Angels who followed Satan
- "Fallen angels free to contaminate the human race with wickedness," (Genesis 3; Matthew 25:41, Revelations 12:9)
- Angels who rebel against God

Godliness:
- Piety or reverence toward God (Youngblood, Bruce, Harrison, 506)
- Result of union with God
- Power from God
- Received God's grace
- Response to God's grace
- Faith in God show or by obedience (Revell Bible Dictionary, Richards, 441)

Godly:
- Holy behavior
- Devout
- Rejects irreligion
- Rejects worldly passion
- Rejects worldly desires
- Lives discreet
- Worshiping God
- Righteous
- Fruit of the Spirit

Rulers and Forces:
- Powerful beings in the unseen world
- Church, spiritual power revealing wisdom of God

# THE ENEMY

The world system is an enemy:[3]
- Invisible system of ideas
- Invisible system of activities
- Purposes of Satan's rule

Sample of invisible system of ideas:
    Issue of Abortion
- When does life begin?
- When is the fetus a human being?

Sample of invisible system of activities:
    Issue of immorality
- Perverted sexual behavior accepted in the world.
- Divorce for any reason accepted in the world
- Adultery accepted
- Remarriage accepted (Matthew 19:1-12)

The Devil, Satan, a Spiritual enemy
The Spiritual Enemy:
- Marshal his army to resist the Lord
- Demonic activity increased by Satan
- The demoniac at Gerasenes had legion (an army) (Luke 8:26-39)
  - Use our emotions against the Lord (Ephesians 4:26)
  - Use personal sins to cause division among Christians
  - Cause physical affliction (Job 2:7)

Demons, Fallen Angels, Satan's Soldiers are Enemies

---

[3] James 4:4 (Amplified): "You [are like] unfaithful wives [having illicit love affairs with the world] and breaking your marriage vow to God. Do you not know that being the world's friend is being God's enemy? So whoever chooses to be a friend of the world takes his stand as an enemy of God."

- Against human beings
- Cause oppression of the Christian
- Possess those who have no faith

(HIV/Aids of the Devil? or of God? STD's of the Devil? or of God? Unrestrained Anger, of the Devil? or of God?)

- Demons, evil spirits (Luke 7:21; Acts 19:12-13)
- Demons, deceiving spirits (1 Timothy 4:1 NIV)
- Demons, spirit of divination (Acts 16:16)

Our Flesh, Our Nature, is Our Enemy
- One's own resources instead of Christ[4]
- The acts of the flesh:
    - Sexual immorality
    - Impurity
    - Indecency
    - Idolatry
    - Witchcraft
    - Hatred
    - Discord
    - Jealousy
    - Fits of rage
    - Selfish ambition
    - Party spirit
    - Drunkenness (Galatians 5:19-21)

(Is the above habitual behavior? You are losing the battle!)

---

[4] Romans 7:18 (Amplified): For I know that nothing good dwells within me, that is, in my flesh. I can will what is right, but I cannot perform it. [I have the intention and urge to do what is right, but no power to carry it out].

Man's heart used by the flesh (Mark 7:21-23)
- Heart, inner self that thinks, feels, decides (Youngblood, Bruce, Harrison, 548)
- Evil thoughts
- Sexual immorality
- Theft
- Murder
- Adultery
- Greed
- Malice
- Deceit
- Lewdness
- Envy
- Slander
- Arrogance
- Folly

(How is your heart?)

# THE BATTLEFIELDS

The Battlefields (Clinton & Hawkins, 233)
- The Mind
- The Heart
- The Mouth

The enemy of the world will attempt to capture the mind:
Fortify your mind
- Desire to obey God's law (Romans 6:33)
- Must think on things by God's standard (Philippians. 4:8)
  - Focus requires effort
  - Focus is an automatic response
  - Focus on what/who is reliable
  - Focus on the honest
  - Focus on what demands respect
  - Focus on the right
  - Focus on the true
- What occupies our mind:
  - Affects speech
  - Affects actions

(Write down what was in your mind during the last week. What thoughts were persistent? What ended in speech? In action?)

## YOUR THOUGHTS

| Pure | Pleasing |
|---|---|
| Moral | Agreeable |
| Chaste | Admirable |
| Lovely | Worthy of Praise |

- Praiseworthy thoughts into practice
  - Moral life
  - Spiritual excellence
- God's truth is pattern for teaching
  - Concepts learned
  - Concepts received
  - Concepts heard

Overcoming arguments against the knowledge of God (2 Corinthians 10:5[5])
- Capture the thoughts
  - Every thought in harmony with Christ's will and ways
    - A struggle
    - Results in victory
  - Must become subject to Lordship of Christ
    - A struggle
    - Result in victory
  - Undermine the thoughts of the enemy
- The Flesh attempts to lead the heart astray
  - Lead away from moral behavior
- Purify your heart (Hebrew 12:15[6])
  - Bitter root, non-Christian virtue
- Apostasy results when we fall short of God's grace
  - Failure to commit to God's grace
  - Missing the mark (Kaiser, 692)
  - Pure heart serves
  - God accepts the pure behavior
  - Serving orphans - pure
  - Serving widows - pure
  - Keep self from worldly behavior – pure

---

[5] "We demolish arguments and every pretension that sets itself up against the knowledge of God, and we take captive every thought to make it obedient to Christ." (NIV)

[6] "See to it that no one misses the grace of God and that no bitter root grows up to cause trouble and defile many." (NIV)

Satan/Demons attempt to influence what proceeds from the mouth (Proverbs 13:3[7])
- Controlling the tongue is a sign of wisdom:
  - Victory
  - Life
  - Death in power of the tongue
    - labels destroy self-image
    - gossip kills character
    - many words lead to sin (Proverbs 10:19)
- Life in power of the tongue
  - Good fruit
  - Avoid calamity (Proverb 21:23)
  - Wisdom[8]
- The tongue difficult to control
  - Control the tongue - control self
  - Control tongue - control behavior
- The tongue corrupts whole person (James 3:6)
  - Tongue source of evil
  - Tongue corrupts person
  - Tongue sets the course

---

[7] "He who guards his lips guards his life, but he who speaks rashly will come to ruin." (NIV)
[8] James 3:2: "We all stumble in many ways. If anyone is never at fault in what he says, he is a perfect man, able to keep his whole body in check." (NIV)

# THE BATTLES
## Light and Darkness

A Battle of Light and Dark
- Inner battle (Psalm 18:28)
- You, O Lord, keep my lamp burning
- Turn my darkness into light
- Presence of the Lord - Light
  - John 3:19
  - Jesus is rejected
  - Love deeds of darkness - evil
  - Jesus is Light
    - Follow Jesus - victory over darkness
    - Follow Jesus - Light for life (John 8:12[9])
  - Jesus rescues from dominion of darkness (Colossians 1:13)
  - The Kingdom of Jesus is Light.

Battle of evil spirits:
- The battle not against flesh and blood (Ephesians 6:12)
- The real enemy is not human opponents
- Human resources can't win the battle
- Stand your ground (Ephesians 6:13-14)
  - Individual Battles [personal and up close]
  - Hand to hand combat

Battle Gear - Armor of God (Ephesians 6:13-17)
- Defensive war clothes to do battle with schemes of the devil
- Defense against governments
  - Defense against powers of evil forces
  - Defense against spiritual forces
  - Protective Gear
  - Wards off evil
  - Belt of Truth
    - No term belt in Greek

---

[9] "Once more Jesus addressed the crowd. He said, I am the Light of the world. He who follows Me will not be walking in the dark, but will have the Light which is Life." (Amplified)

- Action of girt around with truth
- Used to hold leather jacket and skirt of armor (Gower, 20)
- Truth (real) can ward off evil forces
- Truth - God's promises (Romans 15:8)
- Truth - not tainted ( 1 Corinthians 5:8)
- Truth - God's Word (2 Corinthians 6:7)
- Jesus is truth (Ephesians 4:21)
- Teaching the Gospel is truth (Galatians 2:5)
- Truth, a defense
  - Defends against false doctrines
  - Defends against false promises
  - Defends against false gods
- Truth keeps one dressed
- Application:
  - Testimony from participant
  - I believe the promises of God
  - I will stand on His promises
  - I know God will provide
- I know He protects
- I know He heals
- He reveals truth in His word, (Matthew 6:28-33; John 14:13; Psalm 62:2)

- Breastplate of Righteousness:
  - A heart guard
  - A lung guard
  - Greek term is Thorax (Bauer, et al)
  - Protects against any weapon piercing vital organs from front or back
  - Organs vital for life
  - Blood
  - Air
  - Righteousness, God's declaration of imputed righteousness
    - Through Faith (Romans 1:17, 3:21; Genesis 15:6)
    - Imputed from Jesus
    - Righteousness acts in harmony with obligations to God
    - Righteousness acts in harmony with fellow Saints (1 Samuel 24:17)

- Faith is through the heart
- Faith in Jesus, giver of Life (Hebrew 12:2)
- Righteousness is the proclaimed Word
- Righteousness, The Gospel of Jesus Christ (Romans 10:1-13)
- Righteousness, quality of God (Psalm 4:1; Jeremiah 12:1)
  - Application:
    - Participant Testimony
      - Through help of Holy Spirit, will live godly
      - I trust in Jesus Christ
      - Stand for what is right
- Gospel of Peace:
  - Reference on what is on soldier's feet
  - Shoes worn were sandals that had hob nails that could grip the ground
    - Steadiness during combat
    - Similar to football cleats
  - The gospel - glad tidings
    - Good news of Jesus Christ
    - Jesus provided peace
    - Jesus reconciled back to God (2 Corinthians 5:18-20; Romans 5:1)
    - Ability to stand because of salvation that saves (1 Corinthians 15:1-3)
    - Peace from Christ removes fear (John 14:27)
  - Application:
    - Participant Testimony
    - I will spread good news of Christ boldly
    - I will fight the good fight
    - I will run the race
    - I will not be overtaken by fear
    - I will not be overtaken by the struggle
- Helmet of Salvation:
  - Head gear to protect head
  - Head gear to protect ears
  - Head location of perceptual acuity
    - sight
    - hearing

- smell
- Place of hope (1 Thessalonians 5:8)
  - Hope of salvation
  - Perception of our future of eternal life
  - Perception of deliverance from eternal death to life with Jesus Christ (Hebrews 2:1; John 3:16; Romans 6:23)
- The Sword of the Spirit; The Word of God:
  - Spoken Word of God
  - Preached Word of God
  - Guide against disobedience
  - Weapon against temptation
  - Word is Lamp unto our Feet
  - Word is Light unto our path (Romans 10:17, 8:8-10; Hebrews 4:12-13, Psalm 119:105)
  - Application:
    - Participant Testimony
    - I will act by God's Word

Preparation to Use the Armor:
- Prayer in the Spirit
- Being alert (Ephesians 6:18)

## Battle of The Flesh (Romans 6:11-14)

Defeating the Flesh
- In Christ
  - Died with Christ
  - Raised to new life in Christ
  - Dead to sin by Faith
  - Alive to God by Faith
  - Purposefully
    - Not let sin be king in the body
    - Do not give in to evil desires
  - Do not use body for wickedness
    - No prostitution
    - No fornication

- 
  - No pornographic pictures
- Serve God
  - Use body for righteousness
  - Gifts of helps
  - Missions
  - Serving poor
  - Serving needy
  - Serving imprisoned
- Grace enables one to resist power of sin
- Do not follow laws that prevent obeying God (Romans 7:23)
- Gambling addiction (Gambling is an idol)
- Same sex marriage (perversion is sin)
- War in the body
- War between mind and flesh
- Become a casualty - prisoner of battle
- War between good and evil
- Galatians 5:17
  - My flesh desires what the Holy Spirit rejects
  - The Spirit desires what flesh rejects

| FLESH | SPIRIT |
| --- | --- |
| • Pride | • Humility |
| • Material Wealth | • Eternal life & salvation |
| • Erotic Love | • Agape/Philios |
| • Fornication | • Unity in Marriage |
| • Autocratic Leader | • Servant Leader |
| • Life Now | • Patience |

- Defeat the flesh, develop spiritual fruit
  - Live by the Spirit
  - Divine Power
    - All need for life
    - All need for godliness
    - Power in knowledge of Him who called us by His glory (2 Peter 1:3,4)
    - His promises

                - Escape corruption
                - Escape evil desires
        - Battle with Satan
        - Know the spirit (the human person)
        - Every spirit that does not acknowledge Jesus, not from God
        - Spirit of anti-Christ in this world
        - Know, He in us greater than spirit in world - Stand
        - Battle won at the cross (Revelation 12:11) - Stand
        - Firm resistance
            - Resist in power of Christ
        - Cannot resist on own (Revelation 12:11; 1 Peter 5:8-9)
        - Satan can't prevail if resist (James 4:7)
            - Submit to God
            - Be self-controlled
            - Be alert
            - Be firm in Faith

## VICTORY

Winning the Battle
- Submit to Jesus
- Rest in Authority of Jesus over Satan
- Be an overcomer of the World
    - Born of God
    - Have Faith
    - Believe Jesus Son of God (1 John 5:4-5)
    - Have peace in middle of trouble
        - Jesus has over come the world (John 16:33)
        - God permits troubles

Victory over the world - Done deal (1 John 5:4)

# BIBLIOGRAPHY

"Amplified" in *KJV & Amplified Parallel Bible*. Grand Rapids: Zondervan, 1987.

Arndt, William F., Gingrich, F., and Wilbur, A. *A Greek-English Lexicon of The New Testament*, Revised and Augmented by F. Wilbur Gingrich and Frederick Danker; Chicago, IL: University of Chicago Press, 1970.

Barker, Kenneth, General Ed. *The NIV Study Bible, New International Version.* Grand Rapids, MI: Zondervan, 1985.

Brown, Francis, Driver, S.R. & Briggs, Charles A. *Hebrew and English Lexicon of the Old Testament.* Oxford: Clarendon Press, 1930.

Clinton, Dr. Tim, and Hawkins, Dr. Ron *Biblical Counseling Quick Reference Guides.* USA: AACC Press, 2007.

Gower, Ralph. *The New Manners and Customs of Bible Times.* Chicago, IL: Moody Bible Institute, 1987.

Hill, Andrew E. and Walton, John H. *A Survey of The Old Testament.* Grand Rapids, MI: Zondervan, Academic and Professional Books, 1991.

Hunt, June. "Spiritual Warfare" *Counseling Through The Bible.* Dallas, TX.: Hope For The Heart, 2004.

Kaiser, Jr., Walter C., et al. *Hard Sayings of the Bible.* Downers Grove, IL.: IVP Academic, 2007.

Richards, Lawrence O. *The Bible Reader's Companion.* Baltimore, MD.: Ottenheimer Publishers, Inc.1991.

Richards, Lawrence O. *New International Encyclopedia of Bible Words.* Grand Rapids, MI: Zondervan, 1998.

Strong, James, S.T.D., LL.D. *Dictionary of The Hebrew and Greek Words of the Original With References to English Words.* Peabody, MA.: Hendrickson.

Wood, Julia. *Interpersonal Communication, Everyday Encounters,* 3rd ed. Wadsworth, 2001.

Youngblood, Ronald, F., Bruce, F.F. & Harrison, R.K. *Nelson's New Illustrated Bible Dictionary.* Nashville, TN: Thomas Nelson, 1995.

Zuck, Roy B. *Sitting with Job.* Grand Rapids, MI: Baker Books, 1992.

## PART II
## THE HOLY SPIRIT

"You, however, are controlled not by the sinful nature, but by the Spirit, if the Spirit of God lives in you. And if anyone does not have the Spirit of Christ, he does not belong to Christ." (Romans 8:9)

## WHEN TO STOP AND LISTEN
© Brenda Simuel Jackson

When I am going in the wrong direction, the Holy Spirit within sends me a warning signal, **STOP, LISTEN.**

When anger is about to take control, the Holy Spirit within pulls the reigns and says whoa, **STOP, LISTEN.**

When I am confronted with temptations, the Holy Spirit prays the will of my Father on my behalf and says since you don't know what to pray for, be still, **STOP, LISTEN.**

When worldly pleasures began to choke spiritual joys, something within me reminds me of the worldly debt I did not have to pay, **STOP AND LISTEN.**

Jesus Christ sent the Comforter, to guard His investment in me; I need to **stop and listen** to all the spiritual reminders meant just for me.

# THE PERSON OF GOD, THE HOLY SPIRIT
# A NEW BIRTH

I. Tri-unity (The Trinity)
    A. One in unity, three persons
        1. Triunity is composed of three united persons without separate existence so completely united as to form one God
        2. The divine nature subsists in three distinctions: Father, Son, and Holy Spirit
        3. God is three (3) at all times
        4. Each person is equal
    B. There is only one and true God
        1. There are three co-equal and co-eternal persons
        2. The same in substance (nature), but distinct in act of existence
    C. One Person in the nature (essence) of God's isness (subsistence).
        1. Erickson (p. 338), "Remember we cannot fully understand the mystery of the Trinity, even when we see Him, we may not fully comprehend because God is unlimited and we will always be limited, we will never be as God."
        2. "Try to explain it, and you'll lose your mind; but try to deny it, and you'll lose your soul." (unknown)

II. A person cannot be a Christian without the ministry of The Holy Spirit.
    A. The believer is united to Christ by being baptized with the Holy Spirit. "For we were all baptized by one Spirit into one body…we were all given one Spirit to drink." (I Corinthians 12:18)
    B. Since the ascension of Christ, and Pentecost, baptism by the Holy Spirit occurs at the point of belief (in the Gospel).
        1. Acts 1:5 - Jesus said, "For John Baptized with water, but in a few days you will be baptized with the Holy Spirit." (NIV)

2. Ephesians 1:13b-14: "Having believed, you were marked in Him with a seal, the promised Holy Spirit, who is a deposit guaranteeing our inheritance." [The Holy Spirit, our mark of whose we are, our true Spirituality.]
C. The Holy Spirit regenerates, gives birth to the Spirit within the believer. (John 3:5-6)
   1. No one can enter the Kingdom of God unless born of the Spirit.
   2. Spirit gives birth to Spirit.
D. The Holy Spirit indwells the believer. (John 14:16-17) [Jesus told the disciples] "…And I will ask the Father, and He will give you another Counselor to be with you forever - the Spirit of Truth. The world cannot accept Him because it neither sees Him, nor knows Him. But you know Him, for He lives with you and will be in you.] (NIV)
   1. The indwelling of the Holy Spirit is a gift. [Now it is God who makes both us and you stand firm in Christ.]
   2. God anointed us and set His seal of ownership on us
   3. Put His Spirit in our hearts as a deposit guaranteeing what is to come
   4. The believer is indwelled at the moment of true faith. (Ephesians 1:13)
   5. Indwelling is a permanent condition. (John 14:16)
   6. The Holy Spirit is our assurance of salvation.
E. The Holy Spirit gives to each believer gift or gifts for ministry. 1 Corinthian 12:4 -7 There are different kinds of gifts, but the same Spirit. …different kinds of service, but the same Lord. …different kinds of working, but the same God works all of them in all men. Now to each one the manifestation of the Spirit is given for the common good.
   1. One way in which others see the manifestation of the Spirit in the believer is the exercise of Spiritual gift(s).
   2. These Spiritual gifts are the result of grace.
      Romans 12:6 – "We have different gifts, according to the grace, given us." [gifts freely given to meet the needs of the body of Christ]
   3. This gift of the Holy Spirit is used to edify the Church, as Paul states in Ephesians 4:12, "for the equipping of the

saints for the work of service, to the building up of the body of Christ." (NASB)
    4. These gifts from the Spirit are supernaturally derived abilities:
       a. A Spiritual gift is not a place of service.
       b. A Spiritual gift is not an office.
       c. A Spiritual gift is not bound to an age group.
       d. A Spiritual gift is different from a natural talent.
F. The Believing Saint is *controlled* (filled) with/*by* the Spirit.
    1. The Holy Spirit causes the believer to yield to Christ.
    2. Be controlled by Christ
    3. Controlled through the fruits of the Spirit (The new nature)
       a. Love
       b. Joy
       c. Patience
       d. Kindness
       e. Goodness
       f. Peace
       g. Faithfulness
       h. Gentleness
       i. Self-Control
G. The believing Saint needs to be prepared to accept the control of the Holy Spirit.
    1. Preparation to accept the control includes not grieving the Holy Spirit
       a. (Ephesians 5:18) not letting unwholesome talk come from our mouths/ talk that pushes a person down
       b. Not allowing any form of malice to control our emotions (Ephesians 4:29-30)
       c. By not failing to be kind and compassionate
       d. By not failing to forgive
    2. Preparation to accept control includes not quenching the Holy Spirit
       a. Respecting the Spiritual gifts such as prophecies, God's revelation.
       b. The fire within.
    3. The believer controlled by the Spirit is not being controlled by a sinful nature - resisting sin. (Romans 8:9-11)

III. The substance (isness) of the Holy Spirit who resides in each believer and Who is along side of each believer.
   A. The titles of the Holy Spirit are divine, meaning proceeding directly from being deity.
      1. He is called the Spirit of God, being the very person of God.
      2. He is called the Spirit of Christ. (Romans 8:9-11)
   B. Other titles of the Holy Spirit describe His character:
      1. He is called a gift from God
      2. The Holy Spirit is an answer to prayer (Luke 11:11-13)
      3. He is the Spirit of Grace – one who gives unmerited favor and blessings of God to those in which He dwells. (Hebrews 10:29)
      4. He is called the Spirit of burning, of fire as Prophecy by John the Baptist about the time of Pentecost (Acts 2:3), "when they saw what seemed to be tongues of fire..." an indication of an outpouring.
      5. He is the Spirit of Truth (John 14:17), bringing people to the truth of God.
         a. The Holy Spirit lives in the believer.
         b. Christ is in the believer.
         c. Christ is in the Father. (John 14:17-20)
      6. He is the Law of the Spirit of Life, a Controller.(Romans 8:2)
      7. He is the Spirit of the Lord which empowered Jesus Christ with:
         a. Wisdom
         b. Understanding
         c. Counsel
         d. Power
         e. Knowledge
         f. Fear of the Lord
      8. The Holy Spirit of Promise (Ephesians 1:13 NASB) - God's pledge.
         a. Our inheritance
         b. To the glory of God.

9. He is the Spirit of Glory (1 Peter 4:14, Isaiah 11:2, Matthew 3:16) His presence is in all who identify with the name of Christ.
10. He is the comforter (John 16:7 Amplified)
    a. Counselor
    b. Helper
    c. Advocate
    d. Intercessor
    e. Strengthener
    f. Standby
    g. Greek - legal assistant who pleads case, one who applied the atonement.

## CLOTHED WITH THE SPIRIT

I. The person of the Holy Spirit is often called, "The Spirit of The Lords" in the Old Testament, and as did Jesus, the Holy Spirit had a mission.
    A. The Holy Spirit was involved and active in the beginning, in the creation of the world. ( Genesis 1:1-2, 1:26)
    B. The Holy Spirit was active in restraining (holding back) the judgment of the Flood for 120 years.
        1. Noah built the ark
        2. Noah preached that judgment was coming
            a. Genesis 6:6 NIV: The Lord was grieved that He had made man
            b. Genesis 6:3 NIV: Then the Lord said, My Spirit will not contend with man forever, for he is mortal; his days will be hundred and twenty
        3. The Holy Spirit today is holding back the judgment through the Church
    C. In the Old Testament the Holy Spirit also indwelled, but only selected Saints, not as today when all believers are indwelled.
        1. Exodus 31:3, The Lord has a mission, He said to Moses:
            a. Chosen Bezelel… "filled him with the Spirit of God" which provided him special abilities:
                i. skills
                ii. abilities
                iii. knowledge
                iv. wisdom
            b. He was to do God's will, His command
        2. Joshua was described by the Lord as a man in which was the Spirit, and He told Moses to lay hands on him. (Numbers 27:18)
        3. Joshua was being appointed to replace Moses, to lead God's people.
        4. Scriptures does tell us when Joshua was indwelled but Scripture gives us history of his obedience to God's Will, a sign of the Holy Spirit being active in his life.

- a. Numbers 13 & 14 tells of the expedition party sent to survey the land of Canaan that God had given His people.
- b. Caleb and Joshua were the only members of the team who said:
    - i. The land is good
    - ii. If the Lord is pleased with us He will give us the land
    - iii. Pleaded with the people not to rebel against God
    - iv. Pleaded with the people not to be afraid
- c. The people were ready to stone Joshua and Caleb
- d. Moses had changed Joshua's name from Hoshea. Joshua means Yahweh is Salvation, a state of being
- e. Hoshea means Yahweh saves, an action to take place

D. The Holy Spirit clothed (covered), Old Testament saints and enabled them to do God's mission.
1. Clothing the saints was not a permanent indwelling
2. Numbers 11:16-17, 25, The Lord empowered 70 of Israel's elders for leadership.
    - a. The same Spirit of God which rested on Moses, rested on the elders.
    - b. When The Spirit rested on them, the sign was they prophesied, but this was not continuous. (In the New Testament prophecy is a gift of the Spirit. 1 Corinthians 14:1)
3. In the book of Judges, we see the Holy Spirit as the controller, directing the actions of those anointed with the Spirit.
    - a. Judges 6:34 – Gideon was prompted to summon others to follow him into battle
    - b. Judges 3:9-10 – Othniel chosen by God as a deliver for Israel, Scripture says the Spirit of the Lord came upon him, so that he became Israel's judge, went to war, and overpowered the enemy

The Holy Spirit enabled this saint to have physical strength and power. Samson, one of Israel's deliverers, selected from birth, a Nazerite, a person under a special vow to the Lord, one who the Lord chose for a specific assignment. The Spirit of the Lord began to stir him as he grew (Judges 13:24-25). In reading the Scriptures, it is easy to believe that Sampson's strength was in his hair. But not shaving his hair was part of his vow and obedience to God. The vow was broken when his head was shaved; he was no longer set apart. His power was always through the Holy Spirit.

- Judges 13:24-25 – he defeated the lion. The Spirit of the Lord came upon him in power so that he tore the lion apart.
- Judges 14:19 NIV – "Then the Spirit of the Lord came upon him in power… struck down thirty…men."
- Judges 15:14 – "The Spirit of the Lord came upon him in power. The ropes on his arms became like charred flax, and the bindings dropped from his hands."

After he broke his vow, he gained strength because he prayed to God, Who answered his prayer. Not only did the Holy Spirit provide the chosen saints with power and ability to prophesy, the Holy Spirit also changed the chosen one into a different person; reminding us that those who believe, the Holy Spirit changes.

- 1 Samuel 10:6-7 – Saul is chosen by the Lord, Scripture says the Spirit of the Lord will give him power, the ability to prophecy, and change him into a different person, and whatever his hands finds to do will be fulfilled for God is with him.
- 1 Samuel 16:14 – Saul also disobeyed, and failed to please God, and we learn that in the Old Testament the Lord's Spirit would leave one who departed from God's Will; the Spirit of the Lord left Saul.

The Holy Spirit did not just enable leaders and those set aside through a vow, but also clothed the followers in 1 Samuel 19:20 NIV. "So he sent men to capture him. But when they saw a group of prophets prophesying, with Samuel standing there as their leader, the Spirit of God came upon Saul's men and they also prophesized."

The Holy Spirit also guided Old Testament saints in what to say:
- II Samuel 23:2 – The last words of David, "The Spirit of the Lord spoke through me; His word was on my tongue. (David wrote 73 of the Psalms)
- Micah 2:8 – the prophet described how he was able to declare, speak, to Jacob of his transgression – He was filled with the Spirit.
- Zechariah 7:12 describes how prophets received words of the Lord through the Spirit of the Lord.
- Daniel 9:24, Luke 3:21-22 – It was prophesized that the Spirit of the Lord would anoint Jesus the Christ in his humanity. We saw this at His baptism.
  1. Jesus prepared for his mission
  2. Preach the Gospel, Lift the Oppressed, Sight to the Blind
  3. The favorable year of the Lord.

**I. Visions are seen through the Holy Spirit.**

Ezekiel was transported to see future events by the Spirit of God (Ezekiel 11:24). We have seen the activity of being clothed by the Holy Spirit for power, for strength, for prophesizing, for speaking and writing God's Word, being a leader, a follower, and being ready to do God's Will. As we look at Scripture we see the many ways in which the Person of the Holy Spirit of the Godhead is represented:

I. For the believer the Holy Spirit is our clothing.
   A. Luke 24:49 – Jesus is speaking to the disciples; "… you have been clothed with power from on high.
   B. Matthew 3:16 – He is described as being like a dove, as seen when Jesus was baptized and the Godhead was present. (The Spirit of God descending like a dove.)
   C. Ephesians 1:14 – The Holy Spirit is described in scripture as the pledge of our redemption, guaranteeing our inheritance.
   D. Acts 2:3 – His appearance is described like fire in.
   E. 1 Sam 10:1 – The power of the Holy Spirit is described as oil, as Samuel anointed Saul stating, "…has not the Lord anointed you as leader?"
   F. 1 Corinthians 1:21-2 – The Holy Spirit is seen as God's seal of ownership on us and His Spirit in our hearts as a deposit.

        1. God's seal of ownership is The Holy Spirit.
        2. God's authority over the life of the believer is the Holy Spirit living in us.
- G. The Holy Spirit is symbolized in scripture as water, meaning eternal life, "Jesus said speaking of the Holy Spirit who brings salvation to the believer said in John 4:14, everyone who drinks this water will be thirsty again, but whoever drinks the water I give him will never thirst. In deed, the Water I give him will become in him a spring of water welling up to eternal life.
- H. The Holy Spirit is symbolized as wind in John 3:8, when describing the rebirth of the believer. The wind blows wherever it pleases. You hear its sound, but you cannot tell where it comes from or where it is going, so it is with everyone born of the Spirit.

Let us remember the work of Jesus Christ, who died for us, took our judgment, conquered the grave, was resurrected by the Holy Spirit, who ascended into Heaven, and sent The Holy Spirit to bring rebirth, and to grow the body of Christ, the Church, us. Let us walk in the power of the Spirit.

# LIVING BY THE SPIRIT

I. For the believer, The Holy Spirit is our clothing
   A. Jesus speaking to the disciples, "I am going to send you what my father has promised, stay in the city until you have been clothed with power from on high." (Luke 24:49)
      1. Prepared by having access to the power of The Holy Spirit
      2. Prepared through a promise of God, the Father
   B. He is described as being like a dove, Matthew 3:16, as seen when Jesus was baptized and the Godhead was present. (The Spirit of God descending like a dove).
      1. Song of Solomon, a Dove represents the Lover
      2. Ritually a Dove is clean and used as a sacrifice
      3. It was a dove who brought back a sign of restoration to Noah
   C. The Holy Spirit is described in Scripture as the pledge of our redemption, Ephesians 1:14, guaranteeing our inheritance
   D. His appearance was described as like fire in Acts 2:3
      1. Being in God's presence
      2. Being Led by God as was the Children of Israel
   E. The Power of the Holy Spirit is described as oil, as Samuel anointed Saul stating, "Has not the Lord anointed you leader?" (1 Samuel 10:1)
      1. Being prepared for leadership
      2. Being set aside for God's work

II. The work of the Holy Spirit confirms the character of The Holy Spirit Who is in the heart of the believer.
   A. The Holy Spirit teaches. Jesus said, "But the Counselor, The Holy Spirit, Whom the Father will send in my name will teach you all things and will remind you of everything I have said to you." (John 14:25-26)
      1. The Holy Spirit provides for us to live by the Spirit
      2. As Our Counselor, He teaches us
      3. The Holy Spirit guided those who wrote what Jesus said

B. The Holy Spirit testifies, bears witness of Jesus, the Christ, and is our example of what we as students of Christ are to do.
   1. Jesus said in John 15:26, "When the Counselor comes whom I will send to you from the Father, the Spirit of truth." (The Holy Spirit)
   2. He goes out from the Father, He will testify about me, and you [Disciples] must testify for you have been with me from the beginning. (John 15:27)
   3. We are reminded that the ministry of John the Baptist was witness about Jesus
   4. John witnessed, gave testimony about Jesus
C. The Holy Spirit is our Guide (John 16:13) into revealed truth.
   1. Jesus again speaking says, "But when He, The Spirit of Truth comes, He will guide you into all truth,
   2. He will not speak on His own; He will speak only what he hears, and He will tell you what is yet to come."
D. The Holy Spirit convicts, convincing man of sin (John 16:8-11).
   1. "When He [The Holy Spirit] comes, He will convict the world of guilt in regard to sin."
   2. He will convict in regard to righteousness
   3. He will convict in regard to judgment in regard to sin, because men do not believe in Me [Jesus, The Christ]
   4. "in regard to righteousness because I am going to the Father where you can see me no longer,
   5. in regard to judgment because the prince of this world [Satan], now stands condemned."
E. The Holy Spirit enables the believer to have the Mind of Christ.
   1. No eye has seen, no ear has heard, no mind has conceived what God has prepared for those who love Him, but God has revealed it to us by His Spirit (I Corinthians 2:9, 15)

        2.       The Spirit searches all things, even the deep things of God.
        3.       No one knows the thoughts of God, except The Spirit of God.
        4.       The man without the Spirit does not accept the things that come from the Spirit of God, for they are foolishness to him (I Corinthians 2:13-14)
        5.       The spiritual man makes judgments about all things, for who has known the mind of the Lord that he may instruct Him (I Corinthians 2:15)
        6.       But we have the mind of Christ (I Corinthians 2:16)
    F.     The Holy Spirit intercedes (Romans 8:26-27)
        1.       "...the Spirit helps us in our weakness.
        2.       We do not know what we ought to pray for, but The Spirit Himself intercedes for us with groans that words cannot express.
        3.       He who searches our hearts knows the mind of The Spirit, because The Spirit intercedes for the saints in accordance with God's will."
    G.    The Holy Spirit gives commands for action
        1.       Acts 13:2 He says "...Set apart for me Barnabas and Saul for the work to which I have called them."
        2.       Barnabas and Saul were being used on the Mission Field.

III.    Our actions, in-actions, choices, affect our relationship, our living by the Spirit.
    A.    We can grieve the Holy Spirit with sin (Ephesians 4:30)
    B.     Blaspheming the Holy Spirit (Revelations 16:9; Matthew 12:31)
        1.       Refusing to repent
        2.       Refusing to Glorify God
    C.    We can resist the Holy Spirit
        (Stephen told the Sanhedrin in Acts 7:50 "You stiff-necked people with uncircumcised hearts and ears, you are just like your fathers always resist the Holy Spirit.")
    D.    Peter's accusation against Ananias in Acts 5:3, "How is it that Satan has so filled your heart that you have lied to the Holy Spirit?" Yes we can lie to the Holy Spirit.

- E. We, however, can also choose to obey the Holy Spirit. (Acts 10:19-21)
- F. We can quench the Holy Spirit's fire:
  1. Having the wrong attitude
  2. Holding on to evil things
- G. Live by the Spirit (Galatians 5:13-25) allowing His Fruit to be produced in us.

IV. Remember, The Holy Spirit was active in the Life and Ministry of Jesus Christ.
- A. Jesus Christ, in the flesh, was conceived by The Holy Spirit.
- B. Jesus Christ was led by the Spirit into the desert to be tempted by the devil.
- C. The Holy Spirit enabled a sinless offering of blood of Christ. (Hebrews 10:14) The blood of Christ, who through the eternal Spirit offered Himself unblemished to God, cleansed our consciences from acts that lead to death.
- D. The Holy Spirit was the agent of Christ's resurrection (Ephesians 1:19b - 20). That power is like the working of his mighty strength which he exerted in Christ when He raised Him from the dead, and seated him at his right hand in the heavenly realms.

Jesus died so that we could be free from the bondage of sin. He rose that we can have eternal life. The Holy Spirit is our cleansing and controlling Spirit while we live this earthy life, enabling us to live righteously, make right choices, think with the mind of Christ, pray in the Spirit, and show the Fruit of the Spirit in our lives. We must respond to The Holy Spirit in the same manner as to God, The Father, and The Son, in Faith. "We believe God's Word that the Spirit is within us and we rely on Him for the power we need to live holy.

BIBLIOGRAPHY

Barker, Kenneth, General Ed. *The NIV Study Bible, New International Version.* Grand Rapids, MI: Zondervan, 1985.

Erickson, Millard J. *Christian Theology.* Grand Rapids, MI: Baker Book House, 1985.

Thompson D.D. Ph.D., Frank Charles. *The Thompson Chain Reference Bible, New American Standard Version.* Indianapolis, IN: B.B. Kirbride Bible Co., Inc. 1979.

*Seminar 2*
# ALONE IN A CROWDED FISHBOWL

## LONELINESS

BSJ Christian Seminars, Inc.
Minister Brenda Simuel Jackson, Ph.D.
© 2009 All rights reserved.

## ISOLATION
### © Brenda Simuel Jackson

Feel isolated although I can reach out and touch someone.

I feel isolated as I look across the room and notice the work I have done.

I'm not connected to anyone in this place.

I feel violated if someone enters my space.

I feel eyes of rejection constantly following me.

I wish there was trusting confidence I could see.

I heard a small but firm voice say, draw near to me, and hear my Word.

I'll never forsake you or leave you is what I heard.

I need to cast my cares on the One Who can bear,

I need to find a Friend with whom I can share.

In times of loneliness, David found in The Lord genuine concern and no longer was he in deprivation.

I too, in an intimate relationship with my living Savior, will find deliverance from this mental state of isolation.

## FOUNDATIONAL SCRIPTURES:

**Deuteronomy 31:8 (NIV)**
"The Lord, Himself goes before you and will be with you; He will never leave you nor forsake you. Do not be afraid; do not be discouraged."

**Psalm (of David) 25:16-17**
"Turn to me and be gracious to me for I am lonely and afflicted. The troubles of my heart have multiplied; free me from my anguish."

**Ecclesiastes 4:7-12**
"Again I saw something meaningless under the sun"
There was a man all alone he had neither son nor brother.
There was no end to his toil, yet his eyes were not content with his wealth.
'For whom am I toiling,' he asked, 'and why am I depriving myself of enjoyment? This too is meaningless – a miserable business!
Two are better than one, because they have a good return for their work!
If one falls down, his friend can help him up. But pity the man who falls and has no one to help him up!
Also, if two lie down together, they will keep warm.
But how can one keep warm alone?
Though one may be overpowered, two can defend themselves.
A cord of three strands is not quickly broken."

**Hebrews 10:24-25**
"And let us consider how we may spur one another on toward love and good deeds.
Let us not give up meeting together, as some are in the habit of doing, but let us encourage one another - and all the more as you see the Day approaching."

## SEMINAR OBJECTIVES:

- Understand the different types of loneliness.
- Understand the relationship of selfishness with loneliness.
- Understand the physical and emotional aspects of loneliness.
- Model positive methods of combating loneliness.

Biblical Insight to the Scriptures:

I. Deuteronomy:
   A. Last will of Moses
   B. Careful review of the laws of God.
   C. Background Context:
      1. Events from Egypt to the Jordan
      2. Entering the Promised Land
   D. New Generation
      1. Survivors of plague Lord brought to punish 1$^{st}$ generation for sins
      2. Only two of first generation will enter

II. Psalms:
   A. Writing of Psalms span over 1000 years
      1. 1430 B.C time of Moses to 550 B.C written in Babylon
      2. David's Psalms:
         a. Starts 1010 B.C - he began reign in Hebron
         b. Ended 970 B.C he died
   B. Tone of Psalms (Nelson)
      1. Expresses deepest passions of humanity (644-5)
      2. Written in language of human spirit
      3. Utterances of the soul
      4. Takes reader through valleys of human experience
      5. Takes through peaks of human experience
      6. Ends with praise
   C. Psalm 25
      1. A lament
      2. A petition for forgiveness
      3. Emphasis on David's enemies
      4. David retains hope

III. Ecclesiastes:
   A. Theme
      1. All human achievements empty
      2. All human achievements disappointing
      3. Must be something other than human achievement
   B. Theological Contributions

      1. Happiness not in great accomplishments
      2. Happiness not in earthly possessions
      3. True satisfaction in serving God.
      4. Chapter 4 of Book – Inequities

IV. Hebrews
    A. A Book of better things
    B. Theme
      1. Absolute Supremacy of Jesus Christ
      2. Absolute sufficiency of Jesus Christ
      3. Jesus Christ, revealer of God's Grace
      4. Jesus Christ mediator of God's Grace

PRISON LONELINESS (Spitale)
A. A loneliness cannot share
B. Everyone experiences it
C. No privacy but lonely
D. Not alone but lonely
E. Seek Distractions
    1. Letter writing
    2. Poetry
    3. TV
    4. Art
F. Receiving a letter
    1. Letter is real
    2. Says to inmate, You're real
G. No safe person
H. Unknown who to trust
I. Christian Volunteer
    1. Safe
    2. Someone to Trust
J. Seeking comfort
K. Stage of grief
L. Feeling deprived

## Self Assessment

| PART I | YES | NO | DATE |
|---|---|---|---|
| 1. Do you feel alone even when in a room full of people? | ❏ | ❏ | _____ |
| 2. Does the loneliness ever go away? | ❏ | ❏ | _____ |
| 3. If loneliness goes way, what are you doing? | ❏ | ❏ | _____ |
| 4. Have you talked to God about your loneliness? | ❏ | ❏ | _____ |
| 5. Do you feel that God understands your loneliness? | ❏ | ❏ | _____ |
| 6. Do you blame yourself for your loneliness? | ❏ | ❏ | _____ |
| 7. Do you blame someone else for your loneliness? | ❏ | ❏ | _____ |
| 8. Do you remember what has gotten you out of loneliness in the past? | ❏ | ❏ | _____ |
| 9. Do you think past actions will work in this environment? | ❏ | ❏ | _____ |

PART II                                              YES  NO   DATE
1. Do you enjoy being alone?                          ❑    ❑   _____
2. Do you want all things only for yourself?          ❑    ❑   _____
3. Describe the last time you shared something
   material?                                          ❑    ❑   _____

_____

_____

_____

4. Did you share grudgingly?                          ❑    ❑   _____
5. Did you have a real option (choice) not to
   share?                                             ❑    ❑   _____
6. When did you last have genuine fellowship with
   a friend?                                          ❑    ❑   _____
7. When did you write your last letter?               ❑    ❑   _____
8. Do you write poetry or songs?                      ❑    ❑   _____
9. Do you have a legacy?                              ❑    ❑   _____
10. Do you have someone to leave the legacy to?       ❑    ❑   _____

I. What is loneliness?
   A. (Hunt, 04.07/1)
      1. To be desolate
      2. Desert places
   B. (Webster, 498)
      1. Being without company
      2. Cut off from others
      3. Solitary
      4. Sad from being alone
      5. Feeling bleak

II. Types of loneliness (Clinton & Hawkins)
   A. Emotional
      1. No intimate connections
      2. Disconnected
      3. Anxious
      4. Superficial connections
   B. Chronic Loneliness
      1. Persistent feelings of not belonging
      2. Persistent feelings of not being understood
      3. Feelings of worthlessness
      4. Being socially deficient
      5. No hope of connecting again
      6. Deep personal isolation
      7. Deep Despair
         a. Anger
         b. Violent alienation
   C. Spiritual Loneliness
      1. Selfishness
      2. Not content
      3. No friends
      4. No family
      5. No co-workers
      6. No team efforts
      7. Never having enough
      8. Does not fellowship
   D. Situational Loneliness
      1. Physical separation

      2. Emotional Separation
      3. Disruption of intimate relations

III. Nature of Loneliness: (Clinton & Hawkins, 143)
    A. Uncomfortable feeling of isolation
    B. Painful feeling of being disconnected
    C. Feelings of alienation

IV. Physical symptoms of loneliness: (Hunt, 04.07/2)
    A. Headaches
    B. Gastrointestinal problems
    C. High blood pressure
    D. Erratic sleeping habits
    E. Irregular eating habits

V. Differences between alone and lonely:
    A. Loneliness
      1. Emotional feeling of rejection
      2. Negative feelings
      3. Hopelessness
    B. Aloneness
      1. Physical separation
      2. Solitude - positive attributes

IV. Causes of Loneliness:
    A. No one to share joys
    B. No one to share disappointments
    C. Never having enough
    D. Failure to recognize God-given value as a person
    E. Failure to seek God
    F. Failure to establish trusting relationships with others

V. Loneliness of a Solitary Worker (by choice): Ecclesiastes 4:4-12
    A. Critique of work-a-holic
      1. Obsessed with wealth
      2. Forgoes all enjoyment
      3. Dehumanized (Walker, 440)
      4. All alone

         5. Motive is avarice not envy (Ibid)
    B. Selfish greed is meaningless (Scrooge Complex)
         1. One alone minds only him/herself (Henry, 1293)
         2. Cares for no one
         3. Labor motivated by inappropriate incentives
         4. Greed insatiable
         5. Covetousness gives no end to toil
         6. Not content
         7. Person is his/her own center of existence (Clarke, 1293)
              a. No spouse
              b. No children
              c. No legal heirs
         8. Denies self comfort of what one has (Henry, 1293)
         9. Person a slave to business although alone

VI. Those who disconnect with the Body of Christ (Hebrew 10:24-25)
    A. Stops fellowship or gathering with the body
    B. Physical separation
    C. No communion with local gathering

Describe your loneliness. What type of loneliness (if any) are you/have you experienced?

_____

_____

_____

_____


VII. Alleviating, Avoiding Loneliness:
    A. How to cure aloofness, aloneness:
         1. Recognize - God said it is not good to be alone.
         2. Be sociable (Henry, 1293)
         3. Share (Hebrews 2:14)
              a. κοινωνοσ - Share (Vines, 459)
              b. Having something in common
              c. To be a part of

        d. Denotes companion
        e. Share in Christ's glory (Richards, 558)
        f. Being a partner by sharing in Christ
        g. Giving
        h. Fellowship
        1 Timothy 6:18 – Command them to do good, to be rich in good deeds [not things], and to be generous and willing to <u>share</u>.
    4. Exhort: (Hebrew 10:24-25)
        a. Exhortation - to come along side
        b. Exhortation - inspire with truth (Radmacher, 1652)
        c. Urgent need for mutual concern (same today)
        d. Know God is faithful
    5. Fellowship:
        a. Do not abandon meeting together
        b. Don't attempt to defect from your beliefs (Walvoord, 805)
    6. Encourage:
        a. Spur one another to love
        b. Spur one another to do good deeds
        c. Must be considerate of each other
            i. Consider each other's trials
            ii. Consider each other's difficulties
            iii. Consider each other's weaknesses
    7. Godly jealousy:
        a. Watch out for each other
        b. Jealous of ourselves
        c. Jealous of one another
        d. Set examples for others (Henry, 1293)
    8. Endurance

VIII. Action Steps: (Clinton & Hawkins, 145-146)
    A. Recognize feelings of loneliness:
        1. Express the feeling
        2. Write out how you feel
    B. Seek God: (Hebrew 13:5)
        1. Draw close to God; He will draw closer to you.
        2. Get dependent on God not on self

    3. Share communion with someone such as a prayer partner
    4. Listen to Christian and/or inspirational music
  C. Get Involved:
    1. Bible study group
    2. Support group
    3. Sport activity
    4. Community Service
  D. Be Courageous:
    1. Seek trustworthy people
    2. Know God is near

IX. Benefits of Fellowship and Sharing:
  A. Sharing toil
  B. Sharing fruit of toil
  C. Better profit
  D. Help in time of difficulties
  E. Help in time of need
  F. Genuine companionship in human suffering (Teacher's 352 -353)
  G. Fosters love
  H. Fosters good works
  I. Brings perseverance
  J. Provides enjoyment
  K. Brings Christ in the midst of relationships
     "Where two are closely joined in holy love and fellowship, Christ will be. His Spirit come to them...," (Henry, 1293)
  L. Comfort
  M. Intimacy
  N. Relief from problem of isolation
  O. "Fighting the Good Fight!"

## BIBLES

Lockman Foundation. *Amplified Holy Bible* in *Parallel Bible KJV and Amplified.* Grand Rapids, MI: Zondervan, 1995.

Barker, Kenneth, Gen. Ed. *The NIV Study Bible.* Grand Rapids, MI: Zondervan, 1985.

## BIBLIOGRAPHY

Clinton, Dr. Tim and Hawkins, Dr. Ron *Biblical Counseling Quick Reference Guide.* USA: AACC Press, 2007.

Donnelly, R&R & Sons, Compilers. *Webster's Seventh New Collegiate Dictionary.* Springfield, MA: G&C Merriam Co., 1967.

Elwell, Walter A. Ed. *Baker's Commentary on The Bible.* Grand Rapids, MI: Baker Books, 1989.

Henry, Matthew, Jamieson, Robert, Fausset, Andrew, Brown, David, and Clarke, Adam. *The Bethany Parallel Commentary on The Old Testament.* Minneapolis, MN: Bethany House Publishers, 1985.

Hunt, June, "How To Be Alone But Not Lonely," *Counseling Through The Bible.* Dallas, TX: Hope For The Heart, 2004.

Radmacher, Thd., Earl D., Allen, Th.D., Ronald B., and House, Th.D., J.D., H. Wayne. Editors. *Nelson's New Illustrated Bible Commentary.* Nashville, TN: Thomas Nelson, 1999.

Richards, Lawrence O. *The Bible Reader's Companion.* Owings Mills, MD: Ottenheimer Publishers, Inc. 1991.

Richards, Lawrence O. *New International Encyclopedia of Bible Words: Based on NIV and NASB.* Grand Rapids, MI: Zondervan, 1991.

Richards, Lawrence. *The Teacher's Commentary.* Colorado Springs, CO: Victor Books, 1987.

Spitale, Lennie. *Prison Ministry, Understanding Prison Culture Inside and Out.* Nashville, TN: Publishing Group, 2002.

Vine, W.E. Et al. *Vines Complete Expository Dictionary of Old and New Testament Words.* Nashville, TN: Thomas Nelson Publishers, 1985.

Walvoord, John F. and Zuck, Roy B. Eds. *The Bible Knowledge Commentary.* New Testament. Colorado Springs, CO: Victor Books, 1983.

## (SERMON)
## Alone, But Not Lonely

Scriptures:    Hebrews 10:24-25
                Romans 5:5

Argument:    A true Saint may be alone, but is not lonely.
A true Saint has hope through the love of our Savior, Jesus Christ.

Text:    Hebrews 10:24-25:
24. "And let us consider how we may spur one another on toward love and good deeds.
25. Let us not give up meeting together, as some are in the habit of doing, but let us encourage one another – and all the more as you see the Day approaching."

Romans 5:5:
5. "And hope does not disappoint us because God has poured out His love into our hearts by the Holy Spirit, Whom He has given us."

Background:
I. The book of Hebrews:
   A. New Covenant
   B. Better things
   C. Themes:
      1. Absolute Supremacy of Jesus Christ
      2. Absolute Sufficiency of Jesus Christ
      3. Jesus Christ revealer of God's Grace
      4. Jesus Christ mediator of God's Grace

II. Major theme – Plan of Salvation & Righteousness:
III. Chronic Loneliness:
   A. Persistent feelings of not belonging
   B. Persistent feelings of not being understood
      [When with the wrong crowd, should feel lonely!]
   C. Feelings of worthlessness

    D. Social misfit - deficient
    E. No hope of connecting again
       [Sinners may feel this kind of loneliness]
    F. Deep personal isolation

IV. Causes of loneliness:
    A. No one to share joy
    B. No one to share disappointments
    C. Never content with lot
    D. Failure to recognize God-given value as a person
    E. Failure to seek God
    F. Failure to establish trusting relationships with others

<u>Exposition:</u>
I.   Those that disconnect from the body of Christ:
    A.   Stop fellowshipping
    B.   Stop gathering together
    C.   Physically separates from other believers
    D.   No longer shares in communion

II.  Prison Loneliness: (Spitale, 40-44)
    B.   Can't share the loneliness
    C.   Unknown who can trust
    D.   Feel deprived – not punished

III. Avoiding loneliness – even when alone:
    A.   Recognize – God said it is not good to be alone
    B.   Teach yourself to share as Christ shared
        1.   Christ took on flesh to share with humanity:
            a.  Share the feelings
            b.  Share the temptations
            c.  Share physical tiredness and frustration
            d.  Share physical pain
            e.  Share abuse
        2.   We must seek areas of commonality to share
        3.   Learn to be a part of the group
        4.   Share in the glory of Jesus Christ (Your witness)
        5.   Sharing in giving

        a.    Materially
        b.    Spiritually
[1 Timothy 6:18 – "Command them to do good, to be rich in good deeds [not things] and to be generous and willing to share."]
    C.    Exhort others:
        1.    Call to a person
        2.    To Admonish when needed
        3.    To speak with
        4.    To advise
        5.    To encourage
[We are not to forsake assembling, so won't forsake encouraging!]
    D.    Be As Barnabus: (Acts 4:36)
        1.    Name = Son of Encouragement
        2.    Sold his field
        3.    Shared the monies
        4.    An aid to Paul
            a.    Paul rejected by the disciples who feared him
            b.    Barnabus befriended and defended Paul
    E.    Seek mutual concerns, not just selfish interest
    F.    In fellowship:
        1.    Don't leave your beliefs
        2.    Meet with those who have same beliefs
        3.    Draw close to God, He will draw close to you
        4.    Prayer partners
        5.    Listen to Christian music
        6.    Listen to Inspirational music
    G.    Get involved! [In what?]
        1.    Bible Study
        2.    Support group(s)
        3.    Sports
        4.    Community Service [How?]
            a.    Write a service person on active duty
            b.    Be part of a group sponsoring a child
            c.    Study with a partner by mail
    H.    Be courageous
        1.    Seek courageous people
        2.    Know God is near
[Bitterness separates and causes loneliness.]

    I.    "See to it that no one misses the grace of God (falls short).
          1.    Don't let pride cause trouble
          2.    Don't let pride divide (Hebrew 12:15)
          3.    Seek ways to express Agape and Philios love
          4.    Read about Christian role models

IV.    Benefits of fellowship:
    A.    Serving as Christ served
    B.    Sharing in the toil
    C.    Sharing in the fruit of labor
    D.    Help in time of difficulties
    E.    Genuine companionship during human suffering
    F.    Fosters love
    G.    Fosters good work
    H.    Provides enjoyment
    I.    Brings Christ in the midst
    J.    Provides comfort
    K.    Grows intimacy
    L.    Gives relief from isolation

V.    Never spiritually alone
    A.    God's inexhaustible supply of love poured out
          1.    Holy Spirit within us
          2.    Surrounded by God's Love
          3.    Christ in the midst of our fellowship
    B.    Our hope will be fulfilled
          1.    Not unfounded optimism
          2.    Assurance based on God's love
          3.    God has a plan for us.
                a.    He is faithful
                b.    He will never leave or forsake us
                c.    If we walk through the valley of shadow of death, He is there
                d.    In our deserts, He is there
                e.    In sickness, He is there
                f.    In the fire, He is there
                g.    In the flood, He is there
                h.    When we are alone, He is there!

*Seminar 3*
# FEAR AND FAITH

## FAITH FOR FEAR-FILLED DAYS

BSJ Christian Seminars, Inc.
Minister Brenda Simuel Jackson, Ph.D.
© 2009 All rights reserved.

## SEMINAR OBJECTIVES

- Identify our fear(s)
- Identify ways to confront and overcome our fear(s)
- Develop an action plan to overcome the fear(s)

## Faith Filled Fear Days
© Brenda Simuel Jackson

My heart pounded, I could hear and feel each beat.

Sweat drops began rolling down my face from fear's heat.

My mind saw danger everywhere; my eyes were open to peer,

My hands were shaking, my feet felt heavy, a steady pace hard to keep.

I heard my mouth cry, Lord! I heard my mind say, I walk through the shadow of death, that's no lie, then I felt a calming breeze grab my hand, saying I'll walk with you friend.

The pounding in my heart slowed its pace; the sweat drops reduced its running chase.

My Savior in Him, I put my trust and have faith, knowing my fears would diminish in the light of His love and not wanting me my life to waste. I buried my fears in the faithful hands of Him who is ever near. In faith my fear was challenged, and victory was my cheer.

## AGENDA
## Handout

**A.** **Psalm 56:1-13 (NIV)**

    1. Naming our fear(s) on an index card (no personal names)

    2. Exchanging the index cards

**B.** **Defining the terms of fear**

**C.** **Describing categories of fear**

    1. Placing the fear on the index card into a category

    2. Returning the card to its originator

**D.** **Causes of fear**

    1. If know the cause of fear, write it down

    2. If do not know, put cause unknown

**E.** **Methods of overcoming fear**

    1. Develop an action plan

    2. Pray over your action plan with a partner

**F.** **How to be a help during fear filled days**

I.  Introducing our fears:
[Read Psalm 56:1-13 NIV together]
1. "Be merciful to me, O God, for men hotly pursue me; all day long they press their attack.
2. My slanderers pursue me all day long; many are attacking me in their pride.
3. When I am afraid, I will trust in You
4. In God, whose word I praise, in God I trust; I will not be afraid. What can mortal man do to me?
5. All day long they twist my words; they are always plotting to harm me.
6. They conspire, they lurk, they watch my steps, eager to take my life.
7. On no account let them escape; in your anger, O God, bring down the nations.
8. Record my lament; list my tears on your scroll – are they not in your record?
9. Then my enemies will turn back when I call for help, By this I will know that God is for me.
10. In God, whose word I praise, in the Lord, whose word I praise-
11. In God I trust; I will not be afraid. What can man do to me?
12. I am under vows to you, O God; I will present my thank offerings to you.
13. For you have delivered me from death and my feet from stumbling, that I may walk before God in the light of life.

[Instructions: 1. Pass out index cards, 2. Have everyone write down their fear(s), 3. Have attendees exchange cards with a person sitting near them.]
    A. The Psalm records thoughts of David when Philistines seized him in Gath.
    B. Fears that may seize us:
        1. Fear of being alone
        2. Fear of abuse
        3. Fear of abandonment
        4. Fear of being attacked
        5. Fear of cancer

        6. Fear of darkness
        7. Fear of death/dying
        8. Fear of divorce
        9. Fear of failure
        10. Fear of financial loss
        11. Fear of heights
        12. Fear of injury
        13. Fear of being killed
        14. Fear of losing a loved one
        15. Fear of pain
        16. Fear of sickness
        17. Fear of violence

[If you have a fear on the card not on this list, write it on the board.]

    C. The weapon used in the Psalm - Talk
        1. The tongue
        2. Slander
    D. Getting through confessing trust & facing fear
        1. God's promise
        2. Read Psalm 50:15 aloud
        3. Read Psalm 119:74 aloud
    E. Fear because he believes people are conspiring against him:
        1. Calls out to God
        2. God will respond
        3. Have assurance

II. What is Fear?
    A. O.T word – Hebrew ירא - yare
        1. To be afraid - Genesis 3:10
        2. Stand in awe
        3. Psychological reaction
        4. Afraid of something or someone (Vines, 230)
        5. "Cringing fear"
        6. Falling back before superior force in man, animal or God (Richards, 272)
        7. Fearfulness – 1 Timothy 1:7
            a. Coward
            b. Timid (Vines, 230)

- B. Characteristics of Fear:
    1. Normal response to perceived threat
    2. Normal response to real threat
    3. An emotional reaction [Deuteronomy 20:3-4 – Moses encourages Israel not to fear, God is for you]
- C. Fear in New Testament:
    1. Phobos – φοβοσ
    2. Signal to flee
    3. Meaning of flight
    4. Dread
    5. Terror
    6. Concept of dread
- D. Relational Fears: (Clinton & Hawkins, 109-110)
    1. Fears that alter quality of life
    2. Fear of failure
    3. Fear of rejection
    4. Fear of abandonment
    5. Fear of death/dying
- F. Harmful fear is sense of terror (Nelson's Dictionary)
- G. Anxicty:
    1. Constant state of fear
    2. Feelings of unrest
    3. Feelings of dread
    4. Feelings of worry
- H. What a person perceives as real or potential threat to his security

[Summary: (Richards, 272) "We experience fear as fright and also as anxiety about what might happen in the future. God is the antidote for each of these aspects of fear."]

III. Categories of Fear: (Theological Word of the Old Testament)
- A. Emotion – Fear as seen in the Israelites in Deuteronomy 5:5
    1. Afraid to go up the mountain to check out burning bush
    2. Fear - separated from source of protection
    3. Genesis 3:10:

                a.      Adam in Garden, afraid because he was naked – sin
                b.      Vulnerability
                c.      Power of another to do harm
    B.    Intellectual fear of anticipated evil without emphasis on emotional reaction:
        1.      1 Samuel 7:7
        2.      Fear of Philistines
    C.    Reverence and awe
    D.    Righteous Behavior or Piety
    E.    Formal Religious Worship

III.    Causes of Fear:
    A.    May not know root/real cause:
        1.      Need help (counseling) to discover
        2.      Willingness to explore
        3.      May be from past as a child
    B.    Fear of men and what men can do (Deuteronomy 2:25)
    C.    Fear of conditions as in Isaiah 7:25 (like our economic crisis)
    D.    Situational fear as in Jonah 1:10 (fear held by those in the boat)
    E.    Intimidation from worldly – adversaries as in Matthew 10:28 (don't be afraid of those who can kill only the body)
    F.    Fear of superiors
    G.    Fear of anticipated evil:
        1.      Abraham was afraid to say, "She is my wife."
        2.      Abraham anticipated the ruler would want her (Genesis 20:11)
        3.      Saul gripped with fear at size of the Philistine army. (1 Samuel 28:5)
    H.    Fear is lack of trust/faith (1 John 4:18)

## Biblical Accounts of Fear-Filled Days

| SCRIPTURES | CONTEXT | TYPE OF FEAR | ACTION PLAN |
|---|---|---|---|
| Genesis 32:11-13 | Jacob fears anticipating vengeance from his brother Esau | Psychological and Situational | Tried to appease Esau with gifts; Took plight to the promise of the Lord |
| 1 Samuel 21:10-15 & Psalm 34:4 | David is fleeing from Soul and is afraid of the Achish King of Gath, a Philistine, to whose camp he has tried to flee | Relational Fear/Intellectual Fear needed to flee | Pretended insanity; depended on the Lord for delivery |
| 1 Kings 19:1-5 | Jezebel threatens the life of Elijah, who had killed the prophets of Baal | Fear of anticipated evil. | Elijah took flight |
| Isaiah 41:8-10 | Israel is in fear of Cyrus who conquered their captor Babylon | Anxiety, emotional | Rely on the Lord |
| Matthew 14:25-31 | Jesus walks on water, the disciples are terrified, thinking He is a ghost, and Peter walks on water but loses his focus of faith and fears drowning | Emotional Reaction/Relational | Recognize the Lord is with them. Peter calls to the Lord. |
| 2 Timothy 1:7 | Timothy is charged by Paul to oversee the church at Ephesus, and he lacks self confidence that he can do the job. | Relational fear Fear of failure Lack of confidence | Followed the direction of Paul |

Obtain a testimony from one or two participants, using the same approach above.

IV. Action Plans to Control and Overcome Fear(s)
    A. Focus on God (Clinton & Hawkins)
        1. Have a healthy awe of God. (Proverbs 1:7)
        2. Focus on character of God, not on the fear
           (1 Peter 5:7: Cast all your anxiety on Him because He cares for you.)
        3. Focus that God wants us to trust Him.
        4. Focus that God wants us to give our fears to Him.
        5. Reflect on God's strength (Isaiah 26:3) You will keep in perfect peace him whose mind is steadfast because he trusts in You.")
        6. Focus that God is for us & with us. (Richards, 272)
        7. The Lord guards against anticipated evil (Psalm 112:7-10 **read**)
        8. Know that God is in control of our future:
           a. Have hope
           b. Have personal security
        9. Know God is omnipotent:
           a. He releases us from fear
           b. He is faithful to His commitment
    B. Face the fear:
        1. Commit way to the Lord
        2. Wait for the Lord to act
        3. Trust Him
        4. Trusting God focuses our faith
        5. Run to God (Psalm 91:3-6)
        6. Trust God to handle daily difficulties
    C. Replace negative thoughts and lies with the truth of Scripture:
        1. Think on praiseworthy things
        2. Think on the positive not the negative
        3. Read Philippians 4:8
    D. Watch for Triggers:
        1. Minimize activities which induce anxiety
        2. Move forward:
           a. Focus on solutions to problems, not the problem (Matthew 14:22-23)
           b. Seek positive relationships

E. Have patience:
  1. Growth takes time
  2. Reflect on God's grace to provide and to protect
F. Recognize God's plan for us does not include fear
  1. Fear is not trusting God
  2. Fear is not partaking in God's grace (Psalm 27:1)
G. Be willing to analyze fear honestly – discover real source (Proverbs 29:25) "Fear of man will prove a snare, but whoever trusts in the Lord is kept safe.")
H. Be aware of the power of God's love: (1 John 4:18)
  1. Commit to developing faith in God's love Psalm 1:2
  2. Be willing to face situation through faith in the power of Christ.

Challenge yourself to develop your action plan against your fear.

# BIBLIOGRAPHY

## Bibles

"Amplified" in *KJV & Amplified Parallel Bible.* Grand Rapids, MI: Zondervan, 1987.

Barker, Kenneth, General Ed. *The NIV Study Bible.* Grand Rapids, MI: Zondervan, 1985.

## References

Clinton, Dr. Tim, and Hawkins, Dr. Ron. *Biblical Counseling Quick Reference Guide.* USA, AACC Press, 2007.

Harris, R. Laird, Archer, Jr., Gleason L. and Walke, Bruce K. *Theological Wordbook of The Old Testament.* Volume 1 & 2, Chicago, IL: Moody Press, 1980.

Hunt, June, "From Panic to Peace", *Biblical Counseling Keys.* Dallas, TX: Hope For The Heart, 2004.

Richards, Lawrence O. *New International Encyclopedia of Bible words.* Grand Rapids, MI: Zondervan, 1998.

Sherrer, Quin & Garlock, Ruthanne, "Fear vs Trust", *A Woman's Guide To Breaking Bondages.* Ann Arbor, MI: Servant Publications, 1994, 101-127.

Vine, W.E., Unger, Merrell, F. White, William, White, Jr. *Vine's Complete Expository Dictionary of Old and New Testament Words.* Nashville, TN: Thomas Nelson Publishers, 1985.

Youngblood, Ronald F. General Ed. *Nelson's New Illustrated Bible Dictionary.* Nashville, TN: Thomas Nelson, 1995.

*Seminar 4*

# TRAINING UP A CHILD WHILE INCARCERATED

## HOW TO PARENT FROM A PRISON CELL

BSJ Christian Seminars, Inc.
Minister Brenda Simuel Jackson, Ph.D.
© 2008 All rights reserved.

## SEMINAR OBJECTIVES:

- Recognize God's plan for reconciliation with heritage
- Understand the need to re-establish parental relationship
- Overcome limitations created by separation and circumstances
- Identify steps of effective parenting
- Establish methods to facilitate long distance parenting
- To God be the Glory

## BEING SET FREE
### © Brenda Simuel Jackson

My child may reject my desire to a relationship.

But, my child is God's gift to me for my heritage.

My charge is to train up my child as God has planned to be.

Regardless of my circumstances, I must be true to the charge given to me.

I dedicate myself to demonstrate genuine love, and seek my child's forgiveness.

I pray in the name of Jesus, that as He has pardoned me, my child too will set me free.

## Foundation Scriptures

Deuteronomy 6:6-9 (NIV)
6. "These commandments that I give you today are to be upon your hearts.
7. Impress them on your children. Talk about them when you sit at home and when you walk along the road, when you lie down and when you get up.
8. Tie them as symbols on your hands and bind them on your foreheads.
9. Write them on the doorframes of your houses and on your gates."

Psalm 127: 1-5 (Song of Ascents, of Solomon, NIV)
1. "Unless the Lord builds the house, its builders labor in vain. Unless the Lord watches over the city, the watchman stand guard in vain.
2. In vain you rise early and stay up late, toiling for food to eat - for He grants sleep to those He loves.
3. Sons are a heritage from the Lord [favor], children a reward from Him.
4. Like arrows in the hands of a warrior are sons born in one's youth.
5. Bless is the man whose quiver is full of them. They will not be put to shame when they contend with their enemies in the gate."

Proverbs 22:6 (NIV)
"Train a child in the way he should go, and when he is old he will not turn from it."

I. TO PARENT (Verb, Youngblood, 1390)
   A. Physically raise
   B. Emotionally nurture
   C. Spiritually nourish
   D. Serve God
   E. Obey God
   F. To teach (Proverb 1:8,9)
   G. To instruct – "Listen, my son to your father's instruction and do not forsake your mother's teaching..." (Proverb 1:8)

II. TO BE A CHILD (Youngblood, 451)
   A. Obey parents
   B. Honor parents
   C. Respect parents
   D. Respect elders
   E. Do not challenge parents or elders
   F. Jesus expressed love for children
   G. The disciples attempted to keep children from Jesus:
      1. Attitude of times for respect of elders
      2. Cultural issue

III. THE FAMILY (GOD'S IDEAL), (Youngblood, 441-443)
   A. Harmonious
   B. Love for God
   C. Love for neighbor (Deuteronomy 6:6-7)
   D. Traditional Family: (Packer, 440)
      1. Related persons
      2. Living together
   E. Family goals - children grow in godliness (Richards, 263)

IV. ROLE OF A PARENT
   A. Discipline
   B. Guide wisely
   C. Communicate God's Word
   D. Instruct in the Law of the Lord (Deuteronomy 6:6-7)
   E. Patriarchal system, Fathers rule
      1. Father provide Spiritual wellbeing (Genesis 12:8; Job 1:5)

2. Training in godliness (Exodus 12:3, 26-27; Ephesians 6:4)

V. FAMILY RELATIONS DISINTEGRATING (Micah 7:4b-6 [Time of Judgment])
    A. A son dishonors his father
    B. A daughter rises up against her mother
    C. A daughter-in-law against mother-in-law
    D. A man's enemies are members of his own household

VI. FAMILY DEDICATION SERVICE
*(Let each of us dedicate ourselves to God as parents)*
    A. Read Psalm 127:1-5
    B. Read Deuteronomy 5:16
    C. Reread Deuteronomy 6:4-7
    D. Parent's Questions:

*Minister:* Do you as a parent of the child(ren) you bring to the Lord dedicate yourself to providing an atmosphere of reverence for God in this relationship, a spirit of dependence on God in all things great and small, and a consistent exposure of yourself and child(ren) to the Word of God?

*Parent:* Yes, I do

*Minister:* Do you dedicate yourself to providing your child(ren) with assurance of your love and the heavenly Father's love for him/her/them?

*Parent:* Yes, I will

*Minister:* Do you now unreservedly dedicate *(insert the first and middle name of each child here)* to God and promise, in humble reliance upon His grace, to set a godly example for them?

*Parent:* Yes I do, with the help of God.

*Prayer*

VII. FATHER'S SPECIFIC RESPONSIBILITIES IN BIBLICAL TIMES:
    A. Have child circumcised (mark of ownership)
    B. Pass on inheritance to first born
    C. Find a wife for the son
    D. Teach son a trade
    E. Provide for needs of family members
    F. Teach:
        1. Not to borrow unnecessarily - Proverbs 22:7b ( the borrower is servant to the lender)
        2. Not to over spend
        3. To purchase wisely
        4. To depend on God for needs
        5. The commandment not to covet
        6. The commandment not to be jealous
    G. Bring up in the training of the Lord
    H. Bring up in the instruction of the Lord.
    I. Father is principal teacher when male is old enough to work with Father
        1. Need a proxy
        2. Must communicate with proxy
        3. Must get reports of progress
        4. Training programs
        5. Trusted relative
        6. Trusted teacher
    J. Father is not to discourage
        1. Show sin as repulsive
        2. Fulfill your promises
        3. Use scripture to admonish (Proverb 6:9-11)
        4. Perception of earthy father influences child's concept of God. (Matthew 7:11)

VIII. MOTHER'S RESPONSIBILITIES IN BIBLICAL TIMES:
    A. Nursed
    B. Oversight
    C. Kept clean
    D. Training in the formative years (ages 1-5)
    E. Nurture

    F.    Protection
    G.    Comfort
    H.    Protocol of manners as child matured (Youngblood, 428)

IX.    TRAIN UP A CHILD - Proverb 22:6
Purpose of Proverbs
    A.    Frequent references to "my son," emphasis on instructing:
        1.    Instructing the young
        2.    Guiding young into happy prosperous life.
    B.    The verb translated "train":
        1.    Means to dedicate something for service to God (Deuteronomy 20:5, 1 Kings 8:63, 2 Chronicles 7:5)
        2.    Prepare a child for service
        3.    Dedicate the child to God
        4.    Train child for adulthood
        5.    Instruct in the way of wisdom
        6.    Discipline to gain wisdom

[Wisdom is fear of the Lord.]

X.    "When he gets old he will not turn from it" (Proverb 22:66)
    A.    Conforming to God's work
    B.    Conforming to how God has equipped the child (Kaiser, 288)
    C.    Evidence of God's plan for the child [Example Hannah and Samuel]
        1.    Training changes to fit stage of life
        2.    Training changes to fit nature of youth
            a.    Nature - inherent character
            b.    Nature - inborn trait (talent)
            c.    Nature - innate disposition
            d.    I.e. perverse sexuality is against nature (Romans 1:26)
            e.    Normal sexually is natural nature. (Romans 1:26-27).
    D.    Train - to inaugurate "to start an action"
        1.    Start building
        2.    Communicate action
        3.    I.e. Nehemiah building the wall
        4.    Inaugurating the child starts with the dedication (Harris, 301)

5.

XI. TO TEACH IS TO TRAIN UP:
    A. Act of instructing
    B. Giving knowledge
    C. Giving information (Youngblood, 1228)
    D. Yarah (ירה) pointing to fact
        1. Pointing to truth
        2. Proverb 4:4 "he taught me and said, 'Lay hold of My words with all your heart; keep My commands and you will live.'"
    E. Teach, lamad (למד)
        1. Deuteronomy 4:1 teach God's statutes
        2. Deuteronomy 5:1 teach God's laws
        3. Proverb 30:3 teach wisdom
        4. Preserve the faith through your teaching (Vines, 256)

XII. INSTRUCTION IS TO TRAIN UP:
    A. παιδεια paideia,
    B. II Timothy 3:16
        1. A guide
        2. A guardian
        3. A child leader
        4. A tutor
    C. To instruct (παιδευο - paideuw)
        1. Learned behavior (Acts 7:22)
        2. Correction of behavior (II Timothy 2:25)
        3. Discipline

XIII. TO DISCIPLINE IS TO TRAIN UP:
    A. To train by instruction
    B. To control
    C. Positive discipline
        1. Gain knowledge
        2. Gain training
    D. Negative discipline
        1. Punishment
        2. Reproof

- E. παιδευο - denotes training of children
    1. Education
    2. Firm instruction
    3. Goal of salvation (Vines, 97)

## XIX. TO CHASTISE IS TO TRAIN UP
- A. Does not give knowledge
- B. Words of reproof
- C. Word of admonition (1 Timothy 1:20)
- D. Infliction of evil (II Timothy 2:25)
- E. Infliction of calamity (1 Corinthians 11:32; Hebrews 12:6-7, 10; Revelations 3:19)

## XX. THE CORRECTOR (Hebrews 12:9)
- A. Instructor
- B. Disciplinarian
- C. Proverb 3:11-12 – "My son, do not despise the Lord's discipline and do not resent His rebuke, because the Lord disciplines those He loves, as a father the son He delights in."
- D. Hebrews 12:5b-6 – "My son, do not make light of the Lord's discipline and do not lose heart when He rebukes you, because the Lord disciplines those He loves, and He punishes everyone He accepts as a son."

## XXI. THE TRAINER'S PREPARATION:
- A. Receive the compassion of God
    1. Lamentations 3:22,23
        a. The Lord's love keeps us from being consumed
        b. His compassion will not fail
        c. His mercy is new every morning
        d. He is faithful
    2. Lamentation 3:22 - The Lord is good to those who hope in Him
- B. Examine Your Emotions/Motives (Psalm 139:23-24)
    1. Search me, know my heart
    2. Test me, try me
    3. Know any anxiety in me
    4. Eliminate any offensiveness

        5.      Lead me.
- C. Leave the past in the past (Isaiah 43:18-19)
    1. New thing is restoration not condemnation
    2. The Lord makes a way in the desert
    3. Therefore, trust the Lord for a future (2 Timothy 1:12)
    4. Know the Lord will guard
    5. Be not ashamed
- D. Acknowledge your need for the Lord in this matter: (Galatians 2:20)
    1. Know the old life has been crucified
    2. Know Christ lives in you
    3. Know that we live by faith in Christ
    4. Know what Christ has done for us

Seek to build a new relationship with a new foundation with your child(ren)
- E. Establish honesty
    1. Seek to sow good seeds (Galatians 6:7)
    2. Do not mock
    3. Order your life as a pattern one can follow
        a. Bible Study
        b. Obedience (no tickets)
        c. Celibacy
        d. Respected by officers
        e. Respected by other inmates
        f. Honest in assignments
        g. Patient with bunky
- F. Recognize detention is stressful for the child (Balswick, 247)
- G. Establish relationship goals
    1. Objective on which relationship built (remember Deuteronomy 6:6-9)
    2. Seek goals from the child
    3. Pick the right time to intervene into child's life
        a. Birthday?
        b. Special Holiday?
        c. Special event?
- H. Establish a Goel or Kinsman Redeemer – someone who will act as your substitute

        1. Take news to the child
        2. Bring news from the child and environment
        3. The church
        4. Relative
        5. Respected friend
I. Express your love and affection verbally, non-verbally, and in written form
        1. Visitation/hugs, pats
        2. Letters
        3. Cards
        4. Poems
        5. Pictures
        6. Narratives
J. Seek forgiveness
        1. Relationship built on grace
        2. Relationship built on forgiveness
        3. Recognize may not be immediate
K. Make covenant of unconditional commitment (Balswick, 23-27)
        1. Love the child, regardless of your acceptance
        2. Pray for reciprocation
L. Seek to understand the child's environment
        1. Language
        2. Music
        3. Key issues
        4. Idols
M. Witness to your child of your conversion/restoration/life change (Walker, 97-98)
N. Seek to empower the child
        1. To learn
        2. To do
        3. To depend on God
        4. Empowering is action of God in their lives
        5. Empower - build self-esteem
        6. Empower - with appropriate discipline
O. Release the child:
        1. Know when child must make independent decisions
        2. Know when child knows how to use self-control

P. Recognize the sexual issues of your child
   1. Sexuality
   2. Sexual orientation
Q. Help child respond to stress
   1. How to cope
   2. How to problem-solve

## POSITIVE AND NEGATIVE PARENTING IN SCRIPTURE

| Scripture | Child(ren) | Parenting | Training up context |
|---|---|---|---|
| Exodus 2:1-10 | Moses | Hebrew mother; Biological sister | Mother physically nursed and nourished; provided early training and protection; sister kept him connected with biological mother. |
| 1 Samuel 1:21-28; 2:12-26 | Eli's sons Samuel | Eli Hannah | Eli failed to train his sons, and they had no regard for the Lord's Law - resulted in judgment against them and Eli: Hannah dedicated Samuel to the Lord, according to the Lord's plan, and annually provided him clothing. |
| 2 Samuel 13:1-30 | Absalom Ammon Tamar | David | David was distant from his children: he failed to discipline Ammon for raping his half sister, Tamar; result was brother killing brother, and conspiracy against David. |
| Judges 14:1-20 | Samson | Mother Father | Failed to do the fatherly duty of selecting a wife; parents were permissive, and Samson was self-centered and rebellious. |
| 1 Timothy 1:18-19 | Timothy | Paul (Father in the Faith) | Instructed to keep the faith, taught to fight a good fight, and to keep good conscience. |

SELF ASSESSMENT

1. Did you rededicate yourself?

2. How did you reconcile with your child?

3. Did you seek forgiveness?

4. Did you demonstrate love?

5. What did you do to prepare for a parenting relationship?

6. How do/did you communicate?

7. How do/did you teach?

8. How do/did you discipline?

9. How do/did you encourage?

10. How do/did you protect?

11. How are/were you honest and faithful?

PERSONAL TESTIMONIES

# BIBLIOGRAPHY

Barker, Kenneth. General Ed. *The NIV Study Bible, New International Version.* Grand Rapids, MI: Zondervan, 1985.

Balswick, Jack O. and Balswick, Judith K. *The Family.* Grand Rapids, MI: Baker Book House, 1995.

Einspahr, Bruce. *Index To Brown, Driver, Briggs Hebrew Lexicon.* Chicago, IL: Moody, 1976.

Harris, R. Laird, Archer, Hr., Gleason, L. Waltke, Bruce K. *Theological Wordbook of The Old Testament.* Vol I, Chicago, IL: Moody Press, 1980.

Hunt June. "Parenting," *Biblical Counseling Keys.* Dallas, TX: Hope for The Heart, 2004, 1-20.

Kaiser, Jr., Walter C., Davids, Peter H., Bruce F.F. & Brauch, Manfred T. *Hard Sayings of the Bible.* Downs Grove, IL: IVP Academic, 1996.

Packer, J. I., Tenney, Merrill C., White, Jr., Williams. *Illustrated Encyclopedia of Bible Facts.* Vol II, III, Baltimore, MD: Halo Press, 1995.

Richards, Lawrence O. *The Revell Bible Dictionary.* New Jersey: Fleming H. Revell, Co., 1990.

Veech, Dr. Guthrie *Christian Minister's Manual.* Cincinnati, OH: Ohio Standard Publishing, 2006.

Vines, W.E., Unger, Merrill F., and White, Jr., William. *Vine's Complete Expository Dictionary of Old and New Testament Words.* Nashville, TN: Thomas Nelson Publishers, 1985.

Walker, Clarence. *Biblical Counseling with African-Americans.* Grand Rapids, MI: Zondervan, 1992.

Weyman, Dorothy Mason. *Thus Saith God's Word.* N.C.: M.D. Productions, 1998.

Youngblood, Ronald F. General Ed. *Nelson's New Illustrated Bible Dictionary.* Nashville, TN: Thomas Nelson, 1995.

*Seminar 5*

# YOU SHALL NOT MURDER

## (SUICIDE)

BSJ Christian Seminars, Inc.
Minister Brenda Simuel Jackson, Ph.D.
© 2009 All rights reserved.

## I Shall Not Murder
### © Brenda Simuel Jackson

What usefulness is there in me?

The struggle was so great, the end, I could not see.

To be with my Savior was the better place to be.

This life I could stop and to a new life I could flee.

But, this life is not mine to end.

There is hope in living through His strength, I will not give in.

Yes, I was/am tired of the struggle, but in Jesus' custody, I win.

## SEMINAR OBJECTIVES

- Define the different types of suicide
- Describe reasons identified as causes of suicide
- Describe Scriptural situations of suicide
- Clarify the differences between spiritual and physical suicide
- Identify Scriptural answers to battle potential suicide

# You Shall Not Murder

Scriptures: Exodus 20:13;[10] Deuteronomy 30:19[11]
Argument: Man can choose between life and death.
Suicide is a choice.
Suicide is premeditated murder.

I. Definition of Suicide:
    A. Social definition
        1. Suicide equals physical death
        2. Suicide does not equal spiritual death
        3. Suicide is a selfish choice (Proverbs 14:12)
        4. Self-killing does not cause loss of salvation for a "True Christian"
    B. Supported suicide: "Saul said to his armor bearer, 'Draw your sword and run me through." [Saul's desire – 1 Samuel 31:4]
    C. Abuse that leads to death
        1. Use of drugs
        2. Use of Alcohol
    D. Spiritual Suicide, rejecting Jesus
    E. Word Study - רֹאה (To Kill)
        1. (KJV) Exodus 20:13 "Thou shalt not kill."
        2. (NIV) Exodus 20:13 "You shall not murder."
        3. (LB) Exodus 20:13 "You must not murder."
        4. (RS) Exodus 20:13 "You shall not kill."
        5. Connotative meanings:
            a. Noun - murder "...crime of unlawfully killing a person especially with malice aforethought" (Webster, 557)
            b. Verb - "to kill ...a human being unlawfully, with premeditated malice". (Brown, 953)
                aa. To slaughter in brutal manner
                bb. Put to an end

---

[10] NIV, "You shall not murder".

[11] Ibid., "This day I call heaven and earth as witnesses against you that I have set before you life and death, blessings and curses. Now choose life, so that you and your children may live."

- c. To kill:
  - aa. Act of killing
  - bb. Something killed as animal shot in a hunt
  - cc. Enemy destroyed in military action
  - dd. Deprive of life
  - ee. To slaughter - as a hog
  - ff. To veto
  - gg. Cause stoppage
6. Lexical definitions of Hebrew word as used in Exodus 20:13:
   - a. BDB[12] translated murder as slay (Brown, 953)
   - b. Hebrew and Chaldee dictionary - murder - to dash in pieces: (Strong, 78)
     - aa. Put to death
     - bb. To kill
7. Form of root term used in Numbers 35:27, Deuteronomy 22:26, 1 Kings 21:19: involves disobedience:
   - a. Slayer left city of refuge - choice
   - b. Naboth slain to accommodate Ahab's desires
   - c. Judgment for rape
8. Murder with premeditation as in Exodus 20:13, Numbers 35:30, Deuteronomy 4:12; 4:42; 5:17
   - a. Not to kill intentionally
   - b. Does not include accidental actions
9. One who slays or murders as in Numbers 35:6, 11, 12, 16, 17, 18, 19, 21, 25, 26, 28, 30, 31; Deuteronomy 4:42, 19:3, 6; Joshua 20:3, 5, 6; Job 24:14.
   - a. Slays with intent
   - b. Slays without intent
9. To assassinate:
   - a. Intensity of action

---

[12] Francis Brown, S.R. Driver, and Charles Briggs, (eds.) *A Hebrew and English Lexicon of the Old Testament.* Oxford: Clarendon Press.

      b.      Hosea 6:9 bands of robbers lie in wait...murder on way to Shechem....
      c.      Psalms 94:6, "...slay the widow...."
10.    Genre and Literary structure:
      a.      Old Testament:
           aa.    Prohibition from God
           bb.    Shows intent to sin against God
           cc.    Describes accidental acts
           dd.    Subject to punishment
           ee.    Subject to protection where no intent
      b.      φονευω - Greek term used in abstract Exodus 20:15 (13)
11.    Synonyms
      a.      Psalm 10:8, Genesis 4:8
           aa.    To smite with deadly intent
           bb.    Destroy
           cc.    Put to death
           dd.    To kill
      b.      Ezekiel 28:9 – to deadly wound
      c.      2 Kings 14:6:
           aa.    To strike
           bb.    To kill
           cc.    To slaughter
           dd.    A murderer
      d.      Genesis 18:25:
           aa.    To die
           bb.    To kill
           cc.    To destroy
      e.      Job 13:15:
           aa.    To kill
           bb.    To put to death
      f.      Psalm 37:14 – to slaughter
      g.      Jeremiah 50:27:
           aa.    To destroy
           bb.    To kill
           cc.    To decay
      h.      Daniel 2:14 – To slay
      i.      Genesis 43:16 – To slaughter a beast

                j.      1 Kings 10:16-17 – Slaughter as in a massacre
                k.      Genesis 22:10 – Slay for sacrifice.
            12. Antonyms:
                a.      2 Chronicles 20:33 – Devote to religious uses
                b.      2 Chronicles 20:23 – Make accursed
                c.      Jeremiah 40:14 – Vitality
    F.  Use of Hebrew Term:
        1.  Demonstrates justice of God
        2.  Demonstrates establishment of moral system
        3.  Exodus 20:13:
            a.  Applies to those with malice
            b.  Applies to those with forethought
            c.  Applies to those seeking vengeance
            d.  Applies to those who kill accidentally

II. Occurrences of Suicide:
    A.  U.S. statistics of suicide - 2005 data:
        1.  $3^{rd}$ leading cause of death for young between ages 15-24
        2.  $2^{nd}$ leading cause of death for ages 25-34
        3.  $2^{nd}$ leading cause of death among college students
    B.  Michigan Data:
        1.  Rate from 1999-2005:
            a.  11.2 per 100,000 deaths
            b.  $10^{th}$ ranking cause of death
        2.  2006 - 1,049 deaths:
            a.  65+ - 14.7 per 100,000
            b.  4.8 per 100,000 for blacks
        3.  2005 1,108 deaths - ranked $37^{th}$ out of 50 states
        4.  Attempted suicides:
            a.  4,878 recorded annually
            b.  51.6 per 100,000
            c.  Average of 13.4 attempts per day.

III. Factors of risk of suicide (Chaplain Tamrie, V.A.)
    A.  Risk Factors:

       1. Poor self-control
       2. Hopelessness
       3. Recent loss
          a. Physically
          b. Emotionally
          c. Financially
       4. Family history of suicide
       5. History of abuse
       6. Serious health problems
   B. Suicidal Thinking
       1. Threats of harming or killing self
       2. Seeking ways to kill self
       3. Talking or writing about death
       4. Hopelessness
       5. Rage:
          a. Anger
          b. Seeking revenge
       6. Acting reclusively
       7. Feelings of being trapped
       8. Increased use of drugs or alcohol
       9. Withdrawal from social contact
       10. Anxiety
       11. Unable to sleep or
       12. Sleeps all the time
       13. Dramatic mood change
       14. No reason for living

IV. Causes of Suicide
   A. Biblical sketches of suicides:
       1. Avoidance of probable abuse, torture:
          a. Saul - 1 Samuel 31:4,5
          b. Armor bearer would not assist Saul in taking his life
       2. Fear of being murdered:
          a. Saul's armor-bearer
          b. Fear of being left
          c. Died with Saul
       3. Fear of revenge - 2 Samuel 17:23:

                a. Ahilhophel
                b. Fear of revenge for igniting mutiny against David
            4. Fear of humiliation:
                a. Judges 9:54
                b. Abimelech
            5. Taking revenge against oppressors:
                a. Samson - Judges 16:29-30
                b. Killed more in his own dying than in his life
            6. Fear of revenge and being murdered:
                a. 1 Kings 16:18-19 - Zimri
                b. Result of losing the battle
                c. Set place on fire around so he died
                d. He had caused sin
            7. Feelings of remorse for actions
                a. Judas regretted consequences of his betrayal (John 6:70; 17:12; Acts1:18, 25)
                b. Hanged himself
                c. Judas acknowledged sin, but never repented
            8. Fear of penalty for performance - Severe punishment:
                a. Acts 16:27-28
                b. Jailer almost killed himself because thought prisoners under his watch had escaped.
        B. Suicide attractive to desperate people: (Clinton & Hawkins, 254)
            1. Attempt to get out of intolerable circumstances
            2. Way to escape pain of living

V. Responses for Suicide:
    A. Preventive measures in Scripture:
        1. Moses - Numbers 11:14-17:
            a. Expressed suicidal wishes to God (11:14-15)
            b. God intervened with assistance to share Moses burden (Chaplain Tamrie)
        2. Elijah - out of fear for his life expressed wish to die: (1 Kings 19:8)
            a. God sent an Angel

                b.      Elijah received nourishment
       3.      Job - expressed wish for suicide: (Job 7:15)
                a.      Recovered his faith (Job 13:15)
                b.      Did not commit suicide
       4.      Jonah tells shipmates to throw him overboard (assisted suicide):
                a.      God intervenes
                b.      Jonah requests life in the midst of dying
B.      Faith Based model in Suicide Prevention:
       1.      Provide education for mental health
       2.      Foster hope
       3.      Build a support system
       4.      Provide forum for discussion of suicide issues
       5.      Know when to refer to mental health provider
       6.      Gain an understanding of ways to support survivors after suicide
C.      Responses to potential suicide situations:
       1.      Through Christ lead to hope:
                a.      Help acknowledge sin
                b.      Help recognize worth in Christ
                c.      John 3:16
       2.      Remind of God's command not to murder
       3.      Build self-worth:
                a.      Psalm 139:13,16
                        aa.      Recognize self as God's creation
                        bb.      Recognize God has ordained life
                b.      Recognize suicide rejects God's sovereignty (Hunt, 04,02/2-13)
       4.      Accept God's Lordship:
                a.      1 Corinthian 6:19
                b.      Suicide rejects God's sovereignty
                c.      Do not belong to self
       5.      Suicide rejects God's offer of inner peace: (Philippians 4:6-7)
                a.      Anxiousness results from self-centeredness
                b.      Peace of God is inner tranquility causing us to give concerns to God.
                c.      In God's protective custody

6. Recognize our divine power:
   a. 2 Peter 1:3
   b. "His divine power has given us everything we need for life and godliness through our knowledge of Him...."
   c. We are made godly

# REFERENCES

Brown, Francis, Driver, S.R. and Briggs, Charles, A., Eds. *A Hebrew and English Lexicon of The Old Testament.* Oxford: Clarendon Press, 1970.

Carusa, Kevin. "Suicide Prevention, Awareness, and Support," *Centers for Disease Control and Prevention, U.S. Suicide Statistics* (2005), Retrieved 9/23/2009, (http://www.Suicide.org/suicide-statistics,html).

Davidson, Benjamin. *The Analytical Hebrew and Chaldee Lexicon.* 7$^{th}$ Printing, Peabody, MA. 1850.

Gingrich, Wilbur, and Danker, Frederich. *A Greek-English Lexicon of the New Testament and Other Early Christian Literature.* Chicago, IL: The University of Chicago, 1979.

Harris, Laid, Gleason, Archer, and Walke, Bruce. *Theological Wordbook of the Old Testament.* Chicago, IL: Moody Press, 1980.

Hunt, June. "Hope When Life Seems Hopeless," Suicide Prevention. *Biblical Counseling Keys.* Dallas, TX: Hope for the Heart, 2004.

"Michigan Suicide Prevention Fact Sheet," *Suicide Prevention Resource Center.* Retrieved 9/23/2009, 2006 (http://www.suicide.org/suicide statistics.html).

Oliver, Rev. Dr. John P. BCC/ Chief of Chaplain Service. Durham VA Medical Center "Coming Home."

Strong, James. *The Exhaustive Concordance of The Bible.* Peabody, MA. Hendrickson.

Tamrie, Chaplain Alice D. Bonner. "Suicide Ministry," Chief Chaplain Service, McGuire Veterans Affairs, Medical Center, Richmond, VA, 2009.

Vine, W.E., Unger, Merrill, F., and White, William. *Vine's Complete Expository Dictionary of Old and New Testament Words.* Nashville, TN: Thomas Nelson Publishers, 1984.

# Seminar 6
# αγαπαω
# (agape)

BSJ Christian Seminars, Inc.
Minister Brenda Simuel Jackson, Ph.D.
© 2008 All rights reserved.

1 John 2:10-11 NASB

"The one who loves his brother abides in the light and there is no cause for stumbling in him. But the one who hates his brother is in the darkness and walks in the darkness, and does not know where he is going because the darkness has blinded his eyes."

## Love Ya!
### © 2008 Brenda Simuel Jackson

We were young, played til the street lights came on, and hollered at each other, love ya! and went home.

We got older, our paths began to part, but when it was birthday time, we remembered and sent a card, with red roses of love painted on the inside.

We made mistakes along the path of life, we let a birthday slip by, and didn't stop to cry.

The years went, but memories didn't fade; they became more vivid as birthdays were counted that the Lord to us gave.

Out of the blue, one day the phone rang, and you said, hey let's this day together hang.

We hung that day til the street lights came on, we turned and said to each other, love ya, and before going home, we prayed.

## SEMINAR OBJECTIVES

The Participant will:

- Gain an understanding of how love functions in the Bible

- Understand the different characteristics and meanings of the divine, and godly love

- Appreciate the meaning of the truth "God is Love"

- Understand the differences between divine intimacy and human intimacy

- Recognize the similarities and differences between Christian (brotherly love) and romantic relationships

# WORD STUDIES OF THE TERM LOVE

Exodus 34:6-7
הסד (HESED) Love - [A type of loyalty]
I.    Term love associated with constancy and forgiveness.
    A.    Love not a matter of obligation
    B.    Love associated with O.T. grace
    C.    Often translated as compassion
    D.    NIV translates as kindness
    E.    NASB translates as loving kindness
    F.    Hebrew term describes a bond, connection
        1.    Loyalty between relatives
        2.    Loyalty between friends
        3.    Loyalty between allies.

Genesis 22:2 NASB
בּחַ (AHEB) General word for love or like [Relationship]
II.    Term used by God to Abraham: "And He said, 'Take now your son, your only son, whom you love [AHEB], Isaac, and go to the land of Moriah, and offer him there as a burnt offering."
    A.    Used to depict <u>relationship between father and son</u>
    B.    Used to depict special relationship between slave and master (Exodus 21:5)
    C.    Genesis 44:20 "And we said to my Lord...We have an old father and a little child of his old age....and his father <u>loves</u> (AHEB) him.
    D.    This love is like a sign, sample of love between man and God.
    E.    Used in O.T. as love of things, concepts or of unknown people.
        1.    Love for food
        2.    Love for visiting strangers
        3.    Love for wealth (Ecclesiastes 5:9)
        4.    Love of God's command (Psalm 119:4-7, 48, 127.)
            a.    Delight in His commands
            b.    Lifting of hands shows love
    F.    Leviticus 19:18, term used for love of neighbor, a duty, and of self. "You shall not take vengeance, nor bear any

|      | grudge against the sons of your people, but you shall love your neighbor as yourself; I am the Lord." |
|------|---|
| G.   | Same word is used in O.T. when reference human love for God. |
| H.   | Same term used when references God's love of mankind. |
| I.   | The continuum of meaning for the term AHEB |

    1. Meaning ranges from God's infinite affection for His people to carnal appetites of lazy gluttons (Harris, 14)
    2. Love
    3. Like
    4. Be in love
    5. Lovely (adj.)
    6. All derivatives mean love

J. Connotative meanings:
    1. Hosea 8:9 "For they have gone up to Assyria, like a wild donkey all alone; Ephraim as love."
        a. "Ephraim has hired lovers."
        b. Negative connotation (Ephraim sought to buy security, love)
    2. Proverb 5:19: Positive connotation
        a. Picture of a lovely doe
        b. "As a loving hind and graceful doe, let her breasts satisfy you at all times."

K. Bipolar meanings
    1. Pure affections
    2. Impure affections
    3. Divine affections
    4. Human affections (Brown, 12)

L. Strong's dictionary has affections in bipolar areas:
    1. Sexual
    2. Non-sexual
    3. Likes (personal)
    4. Friend as an object (Genesis 27:4)

M. Describes love between human beings - same level

רהמ (RAHAM) Strong Tie

III. O.T. terms designating strong tie between God and His people (children, and His unconditional choice (mercy). (Harris, 842)

    A. Psalm 18:1 "I love (RAHAM) Thee, O Lord, my strength."
    B. Love deeply:
        1. Have mercy
        2. Be compassionate
        3. Root term is from womb (REHEM).
        4. Tender mercy
        5. Compassionate women (NASB) ironic situation -
            a. Lamentations 4:10 "The hands of compassionate women, boiled their own children; They became food for them because of the destruction of the daughter of my people."
            b. Physical needs overpowered emotional love
            c. NIV: "With their own hand, compassionate women have cooked their own children who became their food when my people were destroyed."
        6. Root refers to deep love:
            a. Superior for an inferior
            b. Natural bond.
    C. Has a meaning of - to fondle:
        1. Implied - to love
        2. Implied - to have compassion
        3. To obtain love
        4. To show love

גַּב (EGEB-EH-GHEB)

IV. Term for lust:
    A. To breathe after
    B. To love sensually
    C. To dote on

- D. Ezekiel 33:31 NASB: "And they came to you as people come, and sit before you as My people, and hear your words, but they do not do them, for they do the lustful desires expressed by their mouth...."
- E. Inordinate affection
- F. Sensuous love
  Ezekiel 23:7 NASB: "And she bestowed her harlotries on them, and of whom were the choicest men of Assyria; and with all whom she lusted...she defined herself."
  Ezekiel 23:11 lustfulness

חוק (HESHEQ)

V. HESHEQ - a desire, a things to be attracted, a thing desired:
- A. Solomon emotionally bound to a thing, the Temple, the place
  1. 1 Kings 9:1 NASB "Now it came about when Solomon had finished building the house of the Lord, and the King's house, and all that Solomon desired to do.'"
  2. A love that won't let go (Harris, 332)
  3. Genesis 34:8 - root term - fillets or rings denoting strong desire of man toward a beautiful woman.
  4. Deuteronomy 21:11-14 - Something that attracts
     - a. The one desired whom you married could be released if she did not sexually please her new husband.
     - b. Meaning - something that attracts something or someone. (Harris, 332)
- B. Derivatives (Harris, 332) - center of desire
  1. Desire
  2. Ring clasping a pillar
  3. Furnish with rings
  4. Spoke of a wheel

VI. Love in usage, in O.T., may be divine, neutral, or of a physical nature:
- A. Isaac 'loved' savory meat. - physical

B. Psalmist loved God's commandments (Psalm 119:47) - divine
C. Men can love evil (Psalm 52:3) - physical or ungodly
D. Men can love cursing (Psalm 109:17) - physical or ungodly
E. Men can love good (Amos 5:15) - divine
F. Men can love truth (Zechariah 8:19) - divine
G. Men can love peace (Zechariah 8:19) - neutral
H. Men can love salvation (Psalm 40:10) - divine


New Testament - The Greek Words
I. Agape - "This was a weak word conveying fondness and/or pleasure: (Arndt, 4-5)
   A. The word was given a <u>unique, godly</u> meaning because of the context of the Divine.
   B. αγαπαω (agapao) to love in a social or moral sense without a need of reciprocation.
   C. Matthew 5:43b NASB - "You shall love your neighbor, and hate your enemy."
   D. The term is both a noun, adjective, and a verb.
      1. Matthew 24:12 [αγαπή (noun) "...because lawlessness is increased most people's love will grow cold."
         a. Affection
         b. Benevolence
         c. Feast of charity
         d. Sear love
         e. 114 times
      2. Romans 5:5 NASB - "...hope does not disappoint because the love of God has been poured out within our hearts through the Holy Spirit who was given to us."
      3. As an adjective or noun (αγαπητοσ - agapoetos):
         a. Beloved
         b. Dearly
         c. 63 times

II. The most common word for love in the N.T. is φιξεω (Phileo) and its derivatives:
    A.    A love which develops:
        1.    Indicates fondness
        2.    Develops as persons are attracted to each other
        3.    Relationships built within or outside family context. (Encyclopedia, 420)
    B.    Matthew 6:5 NASB - To be a friend to be fond of [a person].
        "And when you pray, you are not to be as the hypocrites, for they love [fond of] to stand and to pray in the synagogues..."
        1.    Having affection
        2.    Personal attachment
        3.    Personal sentiment
    C.    φιλαδελφια (Wigram, 3):
        1.    Fraternal affection
        2.    Love of the brethren
        3.    Kindness
        4.    1 Thessalonian 4:9 NASB - "Now as to the *love of the brethren* (one Greek word), you have no need for anyone to write to you, for you yourselves are taught by God to love one another."
    D.    φιληδονοσ (PHILEEDONAS):
        1.    Lovers of pleasures
        2.    2 Timothy 3:4 NASB - "treacheorous, reckless, conceited, loverS of pleasure rather than God."
    E.    φιλα γυρια (PHILARQURA):
        1.    Love of money
        2.    1 Timothy 6:10 NASB - "For the love of money is a root of all sorts of evil, and some by longing for it have wandered away from the faith and pierced themselves with many a pang."
    F.    φιλαυτοσ (PHILANITOS):
        1.    Lovers of self
        2.    2 Timothy 3:2 "For men will be lovers of self, lovers of money, boastful, arrogant, revilers, disobedient to parents, ungrateful unholy.

3. covetous
G. φιλανθρωρωσ (PHILANTROPOS):
 1. Courteously
 2. Acts 27:3 NASB - "and the next day we put in at Sidon; and Julius treated Paul with consideration and allowed him to go to his friends and receive *care.*"
H. φιλανθωπια (PHILANTROPIA):
 1. Kindness (Acts 28:2)
 2. Love toward man (Titus 3:4)
I. φιλαδεηφοs (PHILADELPHOS) love as brethren - 1 Peter 3:8 NASB -
 "To sum up, let all be harmonious, sympathetic, brotherly, kindhearted, and humble in spirit."
J. φιλαδελφια (PHILADELPHIA):
 1. "Be devoted to one another in brotherly love; give preferences to one another in honor" (Romans 12:10 NASB)
 2. "Now as to the love [FILADELHFIAS] of the brethren, you have no need for any one to write to you, for you yourselves are taught by God to love [AGAPAN] one another." (1 Thessalonian 4:9 NASB)
    a. Those characterized as with brotherly love were taught to have divine love
    b. Taught by God, all from God is divine
    c. Brotherly love from man
    d. Agape love from God
 3. Hebrews 13:1 NASB – "Let love of the brethren continue" (Man to man)
 4. Since you have in obedience to the truth purified your souls for a sincere love of the brethren (φιλαδελφιαν) fervently love one another from the heart (αγαπησαταε)
    a. The Lord pours into the heart
    b. The love, agape, of the brethren is from God.

5. 2 Peter 1:7 "And in your godliness, brotherly kindness [φιλαδελφιαν], and in your brotherly kindness, love [αγαπην]."
6. φιλανδροσ - Titus 2:4 "that they may encourage the young women to ...φιλανδπουσ love their husband [note not agape], to love their children φιλοτεκνουσ - not agape]."
7. Lover of a good man, lover of good [φιλαγαθον]

III. εποσ (EROS) Love of man and woman:
   A. Not in the Bible
   B. Prevalent in Greek culture
   C. Embraces all aspects of sexual desire

IV. Love and Commitment:
   A. Love may lead to commitment - vice versa
   B. Love is not commitment
   C. Commitment - desire to stay in a relationship

## LIFESTYLE OF GENUINE LOVE

After completing this section on the lifestyle of love, answer these questions:

1. The foundation(s) of my commitment(s) are/is
   _____
   _____
   _____

2. Community is built through
   _____
   _____
   _____

3. Sharing is motivated through
   _____
   _____
   _____

4. Unity is maintained by
   _____
   _____
   _____

5. Name one aspect of your life that gives your life's goal(s) meaning.
   _____
   _____
   _____

6. What provides purpose in your life?
   _____
   _____
   _____

7. The law of relationship is fulfilled through

   _____
   _____
   _____

8. I am spiritually motivated by

   _____
   _____
   _____

9. The better way to confront conflict is with

   _____
   _____
   _____

10. How do we experience the love of Christ?

    _____
    _____
    _____

Deuteronomy 11:1 NASB
"You shall therefore love the Lord your God, and always keep His charge, His statutes, His ordinances, and His commandments."

I. O.T. Love:
    A. Everything God has done in our life is preparation:
        1. To live for Him today
        2. To live for Him tomorrow
    B. Life is love letter to God
    C. Relationship with God is based on trust:
        1. Our love exists because of trust
        2. We experience the love of Christ when we receive love of others

II. Real Divine Love:
    A. Shows a transformed lifestyle:
        1. Love causes believers to act positively
        2. Christians will love even enemies (Richards, 423)
        3. Matthew 5:43-4 NASB – "You have heard that it was said, you shall love your neighbor, and hate your enemy, but I say to you, love your enemies, and pray for those who persecute you."
            a. Divine principle of love
            b. Demonstrates God's love for all mankind
            c. We are channels for God's love (Walwoord, 31)
            d. Goes beyond the Pharisee who taught love only those dear to you.
    B. O.T. commandment:
        1. Love for the stranger visiting the land.
        [Why? Remember you were or will be a stranger.]
        2. Deut. 10:19 NASB - "So show your love for the alien, for you were aliens in the land of Egypt."
    C. Love, a process of evaluating spirituality (1 Corinthians 13:4-7):
        1. Fruit of the Spirit
        2. Description of Christ
        3. Love is always positive

        4. Audience, members of the Corinthian Church
        5. Assessment:
            a. Are you patient?
            b. Are you kind?
            c. Are you jealous?
            d. Are you prideful?
            e. Is your behavior ungodly?
            f. Can you stand negative pressure?
            g. Can you accept being wronged?
            h. Do you rejoice in truth?
            i. What is your response to evil?
            j. Can you remain steadfast in faith regardless of the situation?
    D. N.T. love - A motivator (Readers, 893)
        1. Love of Christ - agape
        2. Unable to truly understand
        3. This love becomes a part of our faith experience
        4. Ephesians 3:16-19 NASB - "That He would grant you, according to the riches of His glory, to be strengthened with power through His Spirit in the inner man; so that Christ may dwell in your hearts through faith; and that you, being rooted and grounded in love, may be able to comprehend with all the saints what is the breadth and length and height and depth, and to know the love of Christ which surpasses knowledge, that you may be filled up to all the fullness of God."
    E. Love strengthens our commitment to live holy. 1 Thessalonians 3:12-13 NASB - "And may the Lord cause you to increase and abound in love for one another, and for all men, just as we also do for you; so that He may establish your hearts unblamable in holiness before our God and Father at the coming of our Lord Jesus with all His saints."

III. Love's Lifestyle:
    A. Love creates community:
        1. John 13:34 - Jesus gives new commandment
        2. Love one another as I have loved you

3. Not as you love yourself

4. <u>Love of Christ</u>    <u>Self-love</u>
   Sacrificial    Self-preservation
   Humility    Prideful
   Faithful    Fickle

   _____    _____

B. Love compels concern for others (agape love):
   1. Spiritual needs
   2. Material needs
   3. 1 John 3:16-18 NASB – "We know love by this, that He laid down His life for us; and we ought to lay down our lives for the brethren. But whoever has the world's goods, and beholds his brother in need and closes his heart against him, how does the love of God abide in him? Little children, let us not love with word or with tongue, but in deed and truth."

C. Love stabilizes relationships:
   1. Philippians 2:2 NASB – "Make my joy complete by being of the same mind, maintaining the same love, united in spirit, intent on the purpose."
   2. Colossians 2:2 NASB – "that their hearts may be encouraged having been knit together in love and attaining to all the wealth that comes from the full assurance of understanding, resulting in a true knowledge of God's mystery that is, Christ Himself."
   3. Love maintains unity in the body (Richards, 422)
   4. God calls us to love Him.
   5. God calls us to love fellow human beings:
      a. 2 Thessalonians 3:5 NASB – "And may the Lord direct your hearts into the love of God and into the steadfastness of Christ."
      b. 1 Peter 4:8 NASB – "Above all, keep fervent in your love for one another, because love covers a multitude of sins."

                    aa.   Love is not blind
                    bb.   Love accepts faults of others
                    cc.   Love is unselfish
    D.   Love provides purpose of life:
         1.   Do not love the world
         2.   If love the world, love is not in him
         3.   Romans 13:10 – love is fulfillment of the law
              a.   Doesn't commit adultery
              b.   Doesn't murder
              c.   Doesn't steal
              d.   Doesn't covet
              e.   Leviticus 19:18
                    aa.   Doesn't take vengeance
                    bb.   Doesn't bear grudge
                    cc.   Loves your neighbor
                    dd.   Does no harm to neighbor
         4.   Only in Christ can a person meet this requirement
    E.   The love of Christ motivates us (2 Corinthians 5:14):
         1.   Love of Christ fills our hearts
         2.   Love of Christ causes us to love others
         3.   Love attributes are godly (1 Timothy 6:9-11)

IV. Spiritual Growth and Love:
    A.   The love of each member holds the church together
         (Ephesians 4:14-16):
         1.   Speaks truth in love
         2.   Grows in Christ
         3.   Proper use of Spiritual gifts
         4.   Grow in love as the body of Christ
    B.   Love needs "genuine spiritual" knowledge of God:
         1.   Insight into God's way
         2.   Love is discerning:
              a.   Selecting the pure
              b.   Not causing others to stumble
              c.   In right standing before God. (Philippians
                   1:9-11 NASB – "And this I pray, that your
                   love may abound still more and more in real
                   knowledge and all discernment. So that you

                may approve the things that are excellent, in order to be sincere and blameless until the day of Christ; having been filled with the fruit of righteousness which comes through Jesus Christ, to the glory and praise of God.")
- C.     Brotherly love (Acts 20:38) suffers pain for a brother.
- D.     Love is aid to resolving conflict:
    1. 1 Corinthians 8:1b-3 – "Knowledge puffs up, but love builds up. But the man who loves God is known by God."
    2. The person who loves opens himself up to God and others. (Disclosure)
    3. The person who loves God, grows spiritually, understands more clearly (Richards, 764)
    4. Opposite of conflict is unity:
        a. Showing love reaches out to the weak
        b. Showing love enables congregations to follow Jesus
        c. Showing love, accepts each other where we are.

[Answer the assessment - Discuss answers]

## εισ τελοσ

## LOVE WITHOUT LIMITS

## Love Is
©2009 Brenda Simuel Jackson

Love rescued me from my sin.

Love redeemed me and made me kin.

Love is faithful and never leaves me to flounder.

Love is a disciplinarian and guides me to recover.

Love is hard to describe but easy to detect.

Love is seen through others as Jesus and the Spirit so selects.

Love has set me free, given me a future, I know I will one day see.

Thank You God for Your love ever existing.

Thank You Lord for Your love ever persisting.

Thank You God that Your love simply Is.

|    | I speak in love: | True | False |
|----|------------------|------|-------|
| 1. | I have selfless concern for another. | ❏ | ❏ |
| 2. | I have a will to love regardless of the quality of the person. | ❏ | ❏ |
| 3. | I am obedient to God's command. | ❏ | ❏ |
| 4. | I have the knowledge of love. | ❏ | ❏ |
| 5. | My actions for others are motivated by love. | ❏ | ❏ |
| 6. | I am not rude. | ❏ | ❏ |
| 7. | I do not rejoice in evil. | ❏ | ❏ |
| 8. | God is love. | ❏ | ❏ |
| 9. | Love never fails. | ❏ | ❏ |

1 Thessalonian 1:3 NIV: "We continually remember before our God and Father your work produced by faith, your labor prompted by love, and your endurance inspired by hope in our Lord Jesus Christ."

I. God's love is not in the material.
    A. AHEB - Hebrew term in O.T. for love also translated like in NIV, love in NASB like in NRSV.
    B. The love of money is vanity Ecclesiastes 5:10 NIV – "Whoever loves money never has money enough; whoever loves wealth is never satisfied with his income. This too is meaningless."

II. Anger does not block God's Love
    A. God's love is forever
    B. God's anger is temporary (Psalm 30:5)
    C. God's love protects from hostility Psalm 36:5-7 - "...Your love, O Lord, reaches to the heavens,...O Lord, You preserve both man and beast. How priceless is Your unfailing love! Both high and low among men find refuge in the shadow of your wings."

[Word for love is translated as mercy.]
        1. Brutal crimes remind us we need to experience God's protective love.
        2. God's love (mercy) is faithful (Psalm 57:1-11)
    D. God doesn't give up: (Hosea 2:19-23)
        1. God acts in love.
        2. God acts in compassion to win us to Himself.
        3. God acts faithfully to win us to Himself.
        4. God acts righteously to win us to Himself.
        5. God acts justly to win us to Himself.

III. God's love has no limits:
    A. Jesus gave everything to keep love going
    B. Jesus loved His own to the end - unchangeable John 13:1 – "...Having loved His own who were in the world, He now showed them the full extent of His love."
    C. John 3:16: "God so loved."
        1. $1^{st}$ century word for love, agape, was weak
            a. Expressed fondness
            b. N.T. writers put in new meaning when used in John 3:16

2. God's giving redefined agape love
   a. Giving His beloved Son for us who didn't deserve such love.
   b. God's motivation for His plan of salvation - Love
   c. Love that gives eternal life
   d. Love that does not condemn.
3. (Richards, 680) "Christ incarnate gives meaning to 'God is love'.
4. Christ crucified gave meaning to 'God is Love.'
5. Agape love is choice:
   a. God chose to love the sinner
   b. God chose to self-sacrifice
6. God's agape love is in Christ
   a. Romans 8:39 – Nothing will separate us from love of God that is in Christ Jesus, our Lord.
   b. Christ is the expression of God's love.
7. Agape love is active, giving - 1 John 4:8-10 NASB – "The one who does not love does not know God, for God is love. By this the love of God was manifested in us, that God has sent His only begotten Son into the world so that we might live through Him. In this is love, not that we loved God, but that He loved us and sent His Son to be the sacrifice for our sins."
8. God is Love:
   a. 1 John 4:6 KJV – "And so we know and rely on the love God has for us. God is love, whoever lives in love, lives in God and God in him."
   b. All that God does expresses His love (Hebrew 12:6)
9. O.T. action of God also based on love continuing
   a. Deuteronomy 4:37-38 – "Because He loved your forefathers and chose their descendants after them; He brought you out of

                Egypt...bring you into their land to give it to you for your inheritance...."
- b. Love alone moved God to choose Abraham
- c. Deuteronomy 7:12-15 "...He will love and bless you..."
- d. The Sinai covenant is called a covenant of love.

  "1 Kings 8:23 – "O Lord, God of Israel, there is no God like you in heaven above or on earth below You who keep your covenant of love with Your servants who continue wholeheartedly in Your way."
  - aa. Repeated in 2 Chronicles 6:14
  - bb. Nehemiah 9:32 "...O our God, the great, mighty, and awesome God, Who keeps His covenant of love..."

D. Love of the Redeemed - (HESED) term uniquely used for the redeemed: (Exodus 15:13)
  1. Redemption result of His love
  2. God has love for the righteous

E. Psalms, love [HESED] associated with God's action toward His people (Richards, 419)
  1. Call to worship (Psalm 5:7, 26:3)
  2. Deliverance from enemies (Psalm 6:4, 17:7; 44:26)

F. In the Prophets, God's love establishes David's throne and kingdom – (Isaiah 16:5) "In love a throne will be established in faithfulness a man will sit on it - one from the house of David."

G. God's love is faithful. Jeremiah 31:3-4 – "The Lord appeared to us in the past saying: 'I have loved you with an everlasting love; I have drawn you with loving kindness. I will build you up again and you will be rebuilt, O Virgin Israel...'"

H. Ultimate love - giving one's life
  1. Martyrs
  2. 1 John 3:16 NASB – "We know love by this that He laid down His life for us."

        3.     We ought to lay down our lives for the brethren.
I.     God's kind of love is from God, shared with us.
        1.     Romans 5:5 "...because God has poured out His love into our hearts..."
        2.     The pouring is by the Holy Spirit Whom God has given to us.
        3.     As God so loved us, we ought to love one another.

## CHRISTIAN LOVE

"Dear Friends, let us love one another for loves comes from God. Everyone who loves has been born of God and knows God."
1 John 4:7

## Brotherly Love/Christian Love

I. Deuteronomy 10:17-19 - Sets the bar high:
   A. God shows no partiality
   B. God accepts no bribes
   C. God defends the cause of the fatherless
   D. God defends the cause of widow
   E. God loves the alien
   F. Love your neighbor as yourself:
      1. Place no limitations upon love for a neighbor
      2. Love to do for a neighbor, what do for self
      3. Neighbor is anyone in contact
      4. Do not seek revenge
      5. Do not bear a grudge
II. Brotherly Love:
   A. David and Jonathon:
      1. Became one in spirit because loved as himself
      2. Friendship endured even though David would replace Jonathon as heir to the throne
      3. Jonathon makes covenant with David because he loved him as himself
      4. Jonathon sealed the covenant by giving:
         a. His robe
         b. His tunic
         c. His sword
         d. His bow
         e. His belt
   B. Lifestyle of Brotherly love:
      1. Love transforms character
         a. Becoming more Christ-like
         b. Righteous in relationships (Richards, 422)
      2. Obedient to God
      3. Love as Jesus loved us.
         a. Limitless love for Christian brothers and sisters
         b. Focus on loving God
         c. Self-sacrifice
III. Communities of Love:

A. Unique society within a pagan culture: (Richards, 704)
    1. Accepts each other
    2. Cares for each other
    3. Supports each other
    4. Encourages each other
    5. Rebukes each other
    6. Honors each other
    7. Committed to each other
B. Those who believe Jesus is the Christ are born of God:
    1. Born of God, love His children (other believers)
    2. Born of God, love Him
    3. Born of God keeps His commands
C. Experiencing God's love takes away fear of Him:
    1. No fear in love
    2. Loves drives out fear
    3. Fear has to do with punishment
    4. If still in fear, not perfect in love
D. God's love is fulfilled on earth when we love others as He loved us. (1 John 4:12 "No one has ever seen God; but if we love one another God lives in us and His love is made complete in us.")

[Priority]
    1. Prayer: May the Lord make your love increase and overflow for each other.
    2. May your love increase and overflow for everyone else.

E. Brotherly love guides our behavior (1 Thessalonians 2:7-9) with and for each other:
    1. Gentleness
    2. Sharing our lives
    3. Sharing our gospel
    4. Worked not to be a burden
    5. Obligation to love others
    6. Leads to acts in harmony with God's commands

F. Obedience - an indication of genuine love for the Lord- Short Test:
    1. Have you taken the Lord's name in vain?

2. Have you worshipped in fellowship?
3. How did you honor your parents?
4. Has you tongue murdered anyone?
5. Have you lusted after anyone?
6. Have you stolen?
7. Have you lied against your neighbor?
8. Are you jealous of the blessings or favor of your brother?
9. Are you harboring anger?
10. How have you loved your enemy?
11. Who have you witnessed to?
12. Did you feed the hungry?
13. Have you prayed for the sick?
14. Did you confess your sins?
15. Did you give the extra coat?
16. Did you give as the Lord as given to you?
17. Did you obey those in authority over you?
18. Did you over eat?
19. Did you cause your brother/sister to stumble?
20. Did you forgive?

F. Love and obedience are so intertwined, you can't have one without the other. (Richards, 691)
1. True obedience is joy-filled reaction to what God did for us through Jesus.
2. John 14:15 – "If you love me, you will obey what I command."
3. John 14:21a – "Whoever has my commands and obeys them, he is the one who loves me."
4. John 14:23a – "...If anyone loves me, he will obey my teaching."
5. John 14:24 He who does not love me will not obey my teaching."

G. Only those in Christ have true agape love:
1. Ephesians 1:12-13 - When separate from Christ, separate from His indwelling love; those once far away, brought near through His blood."
2. Love for God is associated with love for others: (Matthew 22:37-39)

           a.      Our response to God's saving love
           b.      Love God
           c.      Love our neighbor

H. HESED - Love
1. Our free choice
2. Harmonious relationship
3. Appropriate for the relationship (Richards, 418)
    a. Loyalty between relatives
    b. Loyalty between friends
4. Malachi 2:10 - Be faithful to each other
    a. One Father
    b. One creator
    c. Regard everyone as a brother Proverbs 22:2 "Rich and poor have this in common, the Lord is Maker of them all."

I. Degrees of love
1. Bigger sinners, have more to confess and have a bigger love debt.
2. Luke 7:47 – "For this reason I say to you, her sins, which are many, have been forgiven, for she loved much; but he who is forgiven little, loves little."
    a. The self-righteous confess little, love little
    b. The murderer?
    c. The fornicator?
    d. The pornographer?
    e. The abuser?
    f. The liar?
3. Brotherly love was part of creation:
    a. God determined the times and places
    b. Spiritual kinship (Mark 3:34) – Jesus said whoever does the will of the Father is His kin.
4. Brotherly love is concerned about the soul of those served. 2 Corinthians 12:15 NASB – "and I will most gladly spend and be expended for your souls."
5. Brotherly love risk life for others in Christ. - Romans 16:3-4 Priscilla and Aquilla risked their lives for Paul, and for the Gentile church.

6. Jesus' love was fostered in Paul because of His union with Paul.
    a. Philippians 1:7-8
    b. Love in his heart for others on the battle field.
    c. Deep yearning, intense compassionate love
    d. Reaches out to all impartially
    e. Reaches out with no exceptions
7. Brotherly love is fervent (hot, glowing, warming, feeling)
    a. 1 Peter 1:22 - sincere love
        aa. Oobedient to God's trust
        bb. Truth purifies soul
        cc. Results in sincere love for the brethren
    b. 1 Thessalonian 3:12 – Prayer that brotherly love increases toward all men.
        aa. Catholics?
        bb. Muslims?
        cc. Hindus?
        dd. Atheists?
        ee. Neighbor across street?
        ff. Spanish?
        gg. Whites/Blacks
8. Hebrew 13:1-3 – "Keep on loving each other as brothers. Do not forget to entertain strangers, for by so doing some people entertained angels... Remember those in prison as if you were their fellow prisoners...those who are mistreated as if you...suffering."
9. Showing partiality is sin:
    a. James 2:9 – "But if you show favoritism, you sin and are convicted."
    b. The act of love is fulfillment of love principle. (Romans 13:10)
10. Real love is not negative but good. (Romans 12:9) "Love must be sincere. Hate what is evil; cling to what is good."

IV. Christ's love standards:
  A. John 15:12 - Love one another as Christ loved you:
    1. Obedient to God's will
    2. Protective from evil
    3. Sanctified
    4. Interceding
    5. Sacrificial
  B. John 13:35 Others are to know we are disciples of Jesus - how we love each other
  C. Freedom in Christ:
    1. Use freedom to serve in love (Galatians 5:13)
    2. Faith expresses itself in love (Galatians 5:6b)
V. Interpersonal Relations (Ephesians 3:17-18)
  A. Christ is in your heart through faith
  B. Established in love
  C. In togetherness there is power in the love of Christ
  D. We draw on the love of Christ
  E. This love surpasses knowledge.

## ROMANTIC LOVE

- An emotional attraction
- A passionate love affair
- Language
- Prose narrative
- Something which lacks a basis in fact
- Adventurous

## Romance Assessment

- Can you have an emotional attraction without love?
- Have you had a passionate love affair without love?
- Have you used the language of romance without love?
- Have you had a romance based on a lie?
- Have you had a romantic adventure?

How do you describe romance?

# Friendship and Romantic Partners

I. Biblical History:
   A. Bride chosen by parents (Genesis 21:21, 28:1-2).
      1. Many times cousins selected for marriage partners (Freeman, 37)
      2. Eastern custom brides purchased
         a. Dowry is payment for the bride
         b. Dowry compensation to the father
      3. Becoming a wife:
         a. Removal from Father's house
         b. Consummation through intercourse
      4. Betrothal period from days (if widow) to year
         a. Prepare the Bride's dress
         b. Prepare to care for wife
         c. Written contract given with dowry
         d. Espousal is the beginning of marriage period
         e. Communication is through third party - friend of the bridegroom.

II. 20$^{th}$ Century:
   A. Personal choices:
      1. Each person will invest equally in the relationship
      2. Investment (seeking a return on the investment)
   B. Passion:
      1. Positive feelings
      2. Desires for other person
      3. Not restricted to sexual or sensual feelings (Wood, 374)
   C. Commitment:
      1. Desire to remain in the relationship
      2. Is not same as love
      3. Love has a giver and recipient (Wood)
      4. Based on investment put into relationship (Wood, 375)
      5. Extreme commitment can change to obsession (Floyd, 333)
      6. Emotional commitment:

                a. Listening to trivial problems
                b. Spend more time together
                c. Compromise
                d. Generous with praise
                e. Avoid petty conflict
                f. Bound by legal commitments
                g. Bound by financial commitments
            7. When people are committed:
                a. Assume have a future together (Ibid)
                b. Emotional commitment
                c. Sense of responsibility for each other's feelings
                d. Sense of responsibility for emotional well being (Ibid)
    D. Intimacy - abiding affection: (Wood, 376)
        1. High degree of interdependence
        2. What happens to one effects the other
        3. Investment
        4. feelings of closeness
        5. feelings of connection
        6. feelings of tenderness
        7. Warm feelings for another person

III. Styles of Love:
    A. Eros - passionate style
        1. Intense attraction
        2. May include sexual attraction
        3. May be spiritual
        4. May be intellectual attraction
        5. May be emotional attraction
    B. Storge (store-gay) (Wood, 378) [Brotherly]
        1. Comfortable
        2. Even-keeled kind of love based on friendship
        3. Grows gradually
        4. Peaceful
        5. Stable
    C. Pragma love (Wood, 379) [Community, Unity]

        1.     Practical love blends conscious strategies (rules with storge love)
        2.     Security
   D.    Manic love (Wood, 379)
        1.     Passion of eros
        2.     Follow the rules
        3.     Testing
        4.     Unsure
        5.     Seeking to evaluate commitment
   E.    Agape love (Wood, 379)
        1.     Generous
        2.     Selfless
        3.     Puts loved one's happiness above own
        4.     No expectation of reciprocity
        5.     Blend:
                a.     Storge
                b.     Eros
                c.     Love of others
        6.     No personal gain or return (Wood, 380)

Compare romantic love with Brotherly love:

## BIBLES

Barker, Kenneth, Gen Eds *New International Version.* Grand Rapids, MI: Zondervan, 1985.

Scofield, DD., C.I. *The New Scofield Study Bible New King James Version* /Northville, TN: Thomas Nelson Publishers

Thompson, D.D. Frank, Charles. *The Thompson Chain – Reference Bible, New American Standard.* Indianapolis, IN: B.B. Kirkbridebiale Co. Inc. 1979

## BIBLIOGRPAHY

Brown, Francis, Driver, S.R., & Briggs, Charles, A. Eds. *A Hebrew and English Lexicon of The Old Testament.* Oxford: Clarendon Press, 1930.

Edersheim, Alfred. *Bible History, Old Testament.* MA: Hendrickson, 1995.

Floyd, Kory. *Interpersonal Communication, The Whole Story.* New York: McGraw Hill,
2009.

Freeman, James M. *Manners & Customs of The Bible.* New Kensington, PA.: Whitaker House, 1996.

Harris, R. Laird, Archer, Jr., Gleason L. & Waltke, Bruce K. *Theological Wordbook of The Old Testament.* Volume 1&2, Chicago, IL: Moody Press, 1980.

Richards, Lawrence O. *The Bible Reader's Companion.* Ottenheimer Publishers, Inc. 1991.

Richards, Lawrence O. *New International Encyclopedia of Bible Words.* Grand Rapids, MI: Zondervan, 1991.

Strong, James, S.T.D., LL.D. *Dictionaries of The Hebrew and Greek Words of the Original, with References to English Words.* MA. Hendrickson.

Walvoord, John F., and Zuck, Roy B. Eds *The Bible Knowledge Commentary.* Colorado Springs, CO: 1997

Wigram, George V. *The Englishman's Greek Concordance of The New Testament.* MA: Hendrickson Publishers, Inc., 2002.

Wood, Julia T. *Interpersonal communication, Everyday Encounters.* 3rd ed. Wadsworth, 2001.

*Ministry and Board Team Members*

# ABOUT THE AUTHOR

Brenda Simuel Jackson (BA, MA, Master of Divinity, Ph.D. Certified Biblical Counselor), is a born again Christian, affiliated with the Baptist Denomination. She is a member and Minister of New Prospect Missionary Baptist Church, and does ministry through BSJ Christian Seminars, Inc., Prison/Jail Ministry. She is a graduate of Wayne State University, and Moody Theological Seminary – Michigan, formerly Michigan Theological Seminary. She is presently pursuing a second doctorate in Divinity at Jacksonville Theological Seminary with a concentration in prison ministry. She is a member of the pulpit, teaching, and prison ministries of her church.

Dr. Jackson has over thirty years of professional experience in human services, education administration, and management, as well as part-time collegiate instruction. She is currently a part-time faculty member of Wayne County Community College District. She has presented at Conferences of the American Association of Christian Counselors, local church women's retreats, mission programs, Christian Education Institutes, State Correctional Facilities, as well as Professional and Community Programs.

Dr. Jackson is a published writer who released her first book entitled, *A Journey of Redeeming Faith,* in April 2007. It was the first of four seminar compilations entitled, *Reflections on the Path to Wholeness.* The second in the series entitled, *Being Wonderfully Made,"* was released April, 2008, and the third in the series, *Going Through,"* was released in October, 2009. *Cross Roads,* is the last in this series was released in April, 2010. Another book with the same title, *Cross Roads*, is the first in the series, *The On-Going Struggle.* This book is being released in February, 2012. Dr. Jackson also hosted a radio broadcast, "God's Teaching Moments." Her Christian Journey includes short term outreach mission and prison ministry assignments in Japan, South Africa, Jamaica, and Ghana. Dr. Jackson completed prison ministry in Zambia, Africa in December, 2011.

A native Detroiter, Dr. Jackson is a widow, a mother, grandmother, great grandmother, and ninth child of Willie and Lucy Simuel (both deceased). Dr. Jackson is a called minister of the Gospel. Dr. Jackson was licensed as a minister of the Gospel November 13, 2005, and she is an Ordained Chaplain with the International Association of Chaplains. Her vineyard is the prisons of the world.

www.ingramcontent.com/pod-product-compliance
Lightning Source LLC
Chambersburg PA
CBHW052051070526
44584CB00017B/2129